THE SECOND MILE

Because Ordinary Living is Never Enough

BY MIKE HAMAN

Published by Healing Place Productions, Baton Rouge, Louisiana
www.healingplacechurch.org
ISBN-13: 978-0-9788242-1-1
Copyright © 2007 by Mike Haman

All rights reserved under International Copyright Law.
No part of this publication may be reproduced, stored in a retrieval system or transmitted in any form or by any means—electronic, mechanical, photocopying, recording or otherwise—without prior written permission by the Publisher.

Scripture quotations marked (NKJV) come from the Holy Bible, New King James Version. Copyright © 1982 by Thomas Nelson, Inc. Used by permission. All rights reserved.

Scripture quotations marked (THE MESSAGE) come from the Holy Bible, The Message. Copyright © 1993, 1994, 1995, 1996, 2000, 2001, 2002. Used by permission of NavPress Publishing Group.

Scripture quotations marked (AMP) come from the Holy Bible, Amplified Bible. Copyright © 1987, The Lockman Foundation.

Scripture quotations marked (NLT) are taken from the Holy Bible, New Living Translation. copyright © 1996, 2004. Used by permission of Tyndale House Publishers, Inc., Wheaton, Illinois 60189. All rights reserved.

Scriture quotations maked (NIV) are taken from the Holy Bible, New International Version. Copyright © 1973, 1978, 1984 International Bible Society. Used by permission of Zondervan. All rights reserved.

For further information contact:
Healing Place Church
19202 Highland Road
Baton Rouge, Louisiana 70809
or email info@healingplacechurch.org

Printed in the United States of America

*To the amazing people of Healing Place Church:
Your passion to go the second mile inspires me to take what we do to the ends of the earth. The credit belongs to you...The glory belongs to God...And the privilege is all mine! I am honored to serve with you.*

CONTENTS

ACKNOWLEDGEMENTS
FOREWORD

SECTION ONE: THE SECOND MILE p.13
Chapter One - What is the Second Mile?
Chapter Two - Involvement
Section One Laps

SECTION TWO: UPWARD p.45
Chapter Three - Passion for God
Chapter Four - Worship for God
Section Two Laps

SECTION THREE: INWARD p.75
Chapter Five - Courage
Chapter Six - Forgiveness
Chapter Seven - Perseverance
Section Three Laps

SECTION FOUR: OUTWARD p.117
Chapter Eight - Servanthood
Chapter Nine - The Invitation
Section Four Laps

ABOUT THE AUTHOR

Acknowledgements

Success is never singular…it's always the result of the combined effort of many. I have been able to stand on the shoulders of some amazing people who have lifted me to a level I could have never reached on my own. For that, I'm eternally grateful.

Jesus Christ
My life has been forever changed because of His Second Mile love and passion. Apart from Him I am nothing.

My wife, Rachel, and three beautiful children, Alexa, Mikaela, and Trevor
You are my heart and soul. I couldn't ask for a better family to lead, love, and serve. Team Haman is absolutely incredible!!!

My Parents
You gave me roots to anchor my life in Truth and wings to soar above and beyond my wildest dreams. Thank you for always believing in me.

Pastors Dino and Delynn Rizzo
We've taken this journey together for the past twenty years. You have watched me grow up and have encouraged me every step of the way. I would not be who I am today without your input and leadership.

Gayla, Terry, and Johnny
For speaking life into this project and adding value to me personally. If wealth is measured by friendships, I consider myself incredibly rich because of you.

Julio Melara
For taking the time to mentor me, guiding me through the unexplored field of writing. Your values and integrity speak for themselves—because sometimes, the bull wins!

Molly and Jay Venzke
Your time, energy, and giftings brought my raw ideas to a much higher level. Tessa, you were born at just the right time!

Meghan and Kari
Thank you for your eagle eye and for helping me to cross the finish line with excellence.

Brad and David
Without your effort and creativity this message would never have gotten the lift it needed to impact the lives of others. I'm grateful for all you do.

Foreword

BY PASTOR DINO RIZZO

When I first met Mike Haman back in the 1980's, he was a thin, red-headed thoroughbred on the basketball courts at his high school. Today, after more than 20 years of friendship, he's still all those things and more. Most importantly, he's a great husband and father, and he's an incredible blessing to the team here at Healing Place Church. He's a gifted communicator with a passion for scripture and a love for people. God is using him to touch this globe.

In *The Second Mile*, you'll find a message that I believe is exactly what the body of Christ needs to hear today. It is such a simple truth: We are never more like Christ than when we give ourselves to others. Over and over again in Scripture you see this overriding theme to be what God intended for you to be—because there are others waiting in your journey.

I'm completely convinced that when you live your life focusing on your own needs and wants, you miss out on the greatest blessings and joys that life on this earth offers. When you can begin to give away what you wish you had, then you find the abundant life Jesus spoke about.

If you're lonely, be a friend to someone. If your time is limited, volunteer to serve in your church. If your finances are tight, find something to give away. If you're tired of running, go one more mile. Then watch and see what God does in your own life. As you focus on others, you'll find your own life's concerns diminishing and even disappearing. When you extend yourself for others, going beyond what is expected, loving and serving outrageously – that's the sweet spot of life.

I have watched Mike Haman live out the principles he teaches in this book. He is one of the most blessed people I know, and I believe it is because he lives what he teaches. He is a second mile servant in God's Kingdom.

I want to encourage you to not just read this book but to put its principles into practice in your life. It is the core of the Gospel and it is the key to living the life God intended. So lace up your shoes and get ready because you're about to go for a run - a journey that has the potential to change the course of your life if you let it. ENJOY YOUR RUN!

SECTION ONE:
the second mile

"You can make a difference if...
You care more than others think is wise
You risk more than others think is safe
You dream more than others think is practical
You expect more than others think is possible."
—Dr. John Maxwell

CHAPTER ONE

What is the Second Mile?

There has to be more to this Christian life than what I am experiencing, I thought as I was driving home from a time of ministry at a nearby Baton Rouge high school. The moment I realized what I was thinking, my mind answered with, *Wait a minute...I'm a youth pastor! I just had a great meeting with hundreds of teenagers, this is what I breathe air for, the reason I'm taking up space on this earth...I should be feeling fulfilled right now. What is my deal?! Get yourself together, man!* But no matter how much I tried to talk myself out of it, my heart kept coming back to: *There has to be more than this. I mean, what kind of difference am I really making?*

That night several years ago, I have to say the journey home was very disheartening for me. I could not seem to shake the emptiness I sensed on the inside, and yet on the outside, I had everything I thought I wanted. I had a wonderful and dynamic wife, who was also my partner in ministry, I was the youth pastor at Healing Place Church, and was beginning to see positive growth in both the youth and young adult ministries. There was no place else I'd rather be, nor no other 'career' I'd rather be pursuing. Dissatisfaction was the <u>last</u> thing I should have been feeling, but I could not deny its presence gnawing at my gut. I felt half-alive in my spiritual life, and frankly, bored in my Christianity as I walked passionlessly through the motions of ministry. Something was missing, and I was starving for more.

Over the next weeks, I became more determined than ever to pour myself into the ministry. Being a typical guy, I assumed I just needed to 'do' more, conquer more—action is power, right? So over the next few weeks, I rededicated myself to my work at a higher level of commitment than ever before: <u>more</u> study, <u>more</u> energy, <u>more</u> production, HOO-AH! Granted, I did get many projects done during this time, but at the end of the day, I still felt that undeniable sense of dissatisfaction, only now it was coupled with intense physical and mental exhaustion. Frustrated, I did what any red-blooded American man would do…I went to go shoot some hoops. There's nothing like the sound of that leather ball swooshing through the net to help a guy relax. Finally, something tangible I could make some sense out of!

There has to be more than this. I mean, what kind of difference am I really making?

Realizing that simply 'doing more' was not going to fill the tremendous void inside, I decided to take a step back from my career and my works. This reflective time was not only to seek God's face about the inner confusion I was feeling, but also to honestly look at the state of my relationship with Him. What I saw was not very pretty…have you ever seen those old western movies that take place in the middle of an arid desert somewhere, and the only sound heard is the crunching of a tumbleweed rolling across the horizon? As I looked into the scope of my Christianity and relationship with Jesus, there were many accomplishments here and there, along with a very sincere desire to make a difference in the lives of others, but in the distance, I know I saw a tumbleweed roll by.

Determination to discover the answers to the questions rolling around in my heart set in like never before, so I went to the Source, the Light, the only one who can really call Himself "The Man!"—Jesus Christ. When He stepped into our world over 2000 years ago, His footprints only made their marks in a very small patch of our planet, but the sound of those steps are still resonating loudly today. He turned the then known world upside down, and it has never recovered. Jesus has always been my prime role model, and I knew the truth I needed could only be found in Him. I began to carefully study His life and examples so that I could emulate them instead of allowing this root of mediocrity that was trying to settle into my life take hold. As I studied the massive landscape of His teachings, I came across one, seemingly insignificant verse that completely revolutionized my life, my ministry, and my relationship with God.

In the Gospel of Matthew, Jesus preaches one of His earliest messages widely known as the Sermon on the Mount. In it, He makes some outrageous claims as He introduces a new way of living to His Jewish followers—living that requires a love of another kind. Instead of the Jewish approach to life outlined in their Law, like 'an eye for an eye' and 'a tooth for a tooth,' He challenges these men and women to go beyond these formulas, to find within themselves a grace and love like never before. He speaks of a love, not the kind that can be manufactured or produced, but the kind of love that is sparked from God Himself.

He teaches about a generosity that goes beyond what is ordinary, what is expected, as He urges, *"Whoever slaps you on your right cheek, turn the other to him also. If anyone wants to sue you for your tunic, let him have your cloak also."* Then He goes as far as to say, *"Love your enemies and bless those who curse you, do good to those who hate you, and pray for those who spitefully use you and persecute you."* (Matthew 5:38b-40,44, NKJV) I cannot help but wonder what these people so used to a culture of retribution thought of these kinds of concepts.

As I was reading these familiar words of Jesus, I tripped over a small statement sandwiched between the claims listed above that stopped me in my tracks. Tucked away in this skyline of teachings on prayer and possessions, people and promises, motives and desires, I found these red-shaded words: *"And whoever compels you to go one mile, go with him two."* How many times had I read these passages and slid right on by that sentence? What did He mean, 'go with him two?' What did going a 'Second Mile' have to do with everything else he said around it? I was very intrigued...

A quick history of this verse reveals, "At that time, Judea was under Roman military occupation. Under military law, any Roman soldier might command a Jew to carry his soldier's pack for one mile—but only one mile. Jesus says here, 'go beyond the one mile required by law and give another mile out of a free choice of love.'" *(David Guzik's Commentaries on the Bible)* Now I really could not help but wonder what the Jewish people must have thought about this. How could this Man ask of them to serve the Roman soldiers, the very ones who were responsible for their social oppressions, and carry their heavy loads another entire mile when the first one was performed simply out of force and obligation?! That is what I call challenging.

However, before I got too involved in my imaginings of the Jewish people's reactions in Jesus' time, God arrested my heart to apply this concept directly to my own life. Although the example Christ was using of carrying the Roman soldier's pack was only relevant to that particular era in history, this concept of going another mile is a truth resonating beyond the confines of time and culture. By using the illustration of the Second Mile, He is opening up for us a completely new way of thinking, a kind of perspective that totally cuts across the grain of our own human nature and egocentric desires for self-preservation and satisfaction. He is inviting us to rise to a higher standard of life, one that requires service, humility, sacrifice and unconditional love for others. Although I was feeling extremely convicted as the challenge of the Second Mile was penetrating my heart, I could also sense the freedom of breakthrough ready to explode in my life. Yes, the confrontation was a bit painful, but right on its heels was a jubilant excitement for what I knew was going to be the fulfillment of what I was starving for!

MY 1ST SECOND MILE STEP

Our youngest daughter, Mikaela, is a determined little girl, to say the least, and this little bundle of blessing has added an interesting dynamic to our home. If you currently have small children, you know both the joys and challenges they can bring. I'm constantly amazed at her perception of the world—mostly how it revolves completely around her. At three years old, she believed she was the axis upon which the planet and its other existing 6.4 billion inhabitants spun. In her immaturity, she thought Mommy and Daddy were placed in her home as servants to her every whim and desire. Our purpose was to feed her, clothe her, provide shelter for her, bathe her, change her…and most of all, buy her fun things to play with. Sometimes I'd find myself a bit frustrated at her selfishness…until my Father God showed me that as adults, many times our thinking is not much different from my daughter's.

If I'm not careful, more often than not, I can find myself tied up in my own concerns—my schedule, my responsibilities, my problems, my influence, my bills, my health…me, me, me, me, me. "Enough about me, let's talk about you…what do you think about me?" It doesn't take a whole lot of effort to get wrapped up in my own little world. In fact, for most of us, this type of self-concern comes only too naturally. The problem is when we are thinking so much about ourselves all day long, our world shrinks down to a tiny proportion of what God planned for us…along with our Christianity, and any impact we ever planned to make on this earth.

As I began to understand the concept of the Second Mile, I recognized the reason I had been experiencing such a deep dissatisfaction in my heart was simply because of a lack of focus upon the needs of the hurting people around me. It was not until I began to take my eyes off of myself, to open my life to opportunities to share the love of God through service, that I began to experience an excitement and fulfillment in my life beyond what I could ever have imagined. My first step into the Second Mile life all began with Coach Montgomery.

Coach Montgomery was a tough, football coach who worked at a local high school, and whom I had met through my work with teenagers and campus ministry. I had never had a conversation with him about where he stood with Christ, but the students absolutely loved him. His love and passion for each and every one of them was like a magnet, and those teens would do anything for this man. Because I was a focused athlete in high school and college, Coach and I made an immediate connection, and I looked forward to seeing him every week when I ministered at his high school.

> **When we think about ourselves all day long, our world shrinks down to a tiny proportion of what God planned for us.**

A few months later, on Thanksgiving day, as I was getting dressed and preparing to spend the holiday with my family, my mouth-watering visions of my wife's homemade cornbread dressing were interrupted by a stray thought…"Coach." Like a flash of lightening, his face popped into my head. *I wonder what he's doing today*, I thought and left it at that. Or at least I tried to leave it at that. I couldn't shake the impulse that I should call him. I tried to negotiate with God. "Lord, please, not today. It's a holiday and I'd love to spend it uninterrupted with my family. Can't we just put ministry on hold just this once? I've got some serious eating to do, and I'm sure Coach doesn't want to be interrupted from his family today either!"

Ever try to bargain with God? It only takes a moment to realize He always has the upper hand. I knew that I could not completely enjoy my Chocolate Chess pie, or my time on the sofa watching the Dallas Cowboys play football through the haze of my self-induced turkey coma until I obeyed God. A bit reluctant, I made the call. When the answering machine picked up, I admit I was relieved, and I left a message.

"Hey, Coach! This is Mike. I know it's Thanksgiving today, but I couldn't get you off my mind. Just want you to know that I am very thankful for you in my life, and I hope you and your family are having a great day." Assignment complete—it's turkey time!

The next time I saw Coach, he surprised me with some shocking news. "I got your message last week," he said, "and I want you to know I really appreciated your call. Over the holiday, my wife and her mother were involved in a terrible car accident. My wife was pretty banged up, but she's going to be alright. Her mother, on the other hand, suffered severe injuries, and the doctors are not sure if she will ever walk again. My wife is going to have to quit her job in order to take care of her, and I had to pick up a second job in order to make ends meet. Sometimes I don't get home until 2 am, and I've been pretty tired. Your phone call really lifted my spirits. Thanks so much."

I was speechless (kind of a miracle in itself, actually), and was very grateful that I had listened to God and made that call on Thanksgiving. I tried to be of some encouragement to him, but as I left school that day, my heart was heavy for Coach and his family. How quickly we can be blind-sided by tragedy; a crisis can happen instantly, giving us no time to prepare. I prayed that God would meet all their needs physically, emotionally, and financially.

Several weeks later, I was unable to sleep, so I decided to use the time to run a few midnight errands. As I was driving through the city of Baton Rouge, feeling like I was one of the only people awake, my mind began to revisit those big questions: *Am I really making a difference with my life? Why can't I shake off this nagging feeling of dissatisfaction?*

Bam! Once again, like a bolt of lightening, Coach's face came to my mind. I replayed our last conversation, how he had to start a second job that kept him out until 2 am, and how downcast his face was that day. Suddenly, I remembered the name of the place he said he worked; it was a restaurant and bar not far from my house. The pieces of the puzzle were coming together—Coach had been moonlighting as a bartender. *What a bummer!* I thought.

As I was making my way home, my clock radio reading 1:30 am, I felt a spiritual impulse telling me to pull over and see if Coach was working his night shift at the bar. At first, I began to rebuke the evil spirit that suggested such a thought to my mind, but very soon, I realized the source was coming from quite the opposite direction. My heart began to race, and my palms started sweating. Certainly, God was not asking me to stop now!

"There is no way I can do that, God!" I reasoned. "I'm a pastor in this community...a youth pastor with lots of young men counting on me and looking up to me. I have a reputation to uphold. What if someone sees me going into this bar and thinks I'm stopping in to throw back a few cold ones? My job, my credibility, my future...." Once again, there was the bargaining with God, and once again, there He was with the upper hand. Clearly I was talking, but I'm sure all He was hearing was, "blah, blah, blah..."

*You've been talking to Me about how you want your life to make a difference...*I felt God speaking to my heart, *Well, I'm giving you an opportunity here, to go deeper with Me. Take it or leave it.*

Bold love requires us to go out to the edge to reach people on the edge. At that moment, I felt as though I was facing a crossroads. I had been 'playing it safe' as a Christian all my life, and now God was challenging me to take a risk, to step out of my comfort zone, and to believe Him for the results. Then I remembered the scripture that had been rolling around in my heart, *"Whoever compels you to go with him one mile, go two."* Was this what Jesus was talking about? Is this what He meant by going a Second Mile? I felt emboldened, and knew I did not want to blow this chance God had offered me to make a difference in this man's life. I swerved my car into the parking lot, took a deep breath, and whispered, "Okay, God...let's roll!"

I walked into that bar as if I owned the place and quickly scanned the room. I saw a handful of guys smoking and talking in the corner, but no Coach. I turned to the left and locked eyes with the man behind the bar. "Coach!" I yelled. "Whassssup?!!!!"

His jaw dropped. "Mike, what in the world are you doing here?"

I said casually, "Oh, I was just running a few midnight errands, and I thought I would drop by to say, 'Hi.'"

"I can't believe you would come in here to see me," he said in amazement.

"Well, to tell you the truth, Coach, I don't know why, and I can't explain this, but I'm losing sleep over you. I know we're supposed to be men—rugged, tough, macho—but I believe God wants me to reach out to you. Ever since you told me about your family situation and how difficult things are at your house right now, I have been thinking of ways I might help. Please, can I come over and cut your grass, maybe pick up some groceries, cook you a meal—and when I say, 'cook you a meal,' of course I mean have my wife cook you a meal. What can I do to help you out?"

> **Bold love requires us to go out to the edge to reach people on the edge.**

Even in the dim light of the bar, I could see tears beginning to fill his eyes.

"Can we go outside and talk?" he asked.

For the next thirty minutes, Coach opened wide his life: his discouragements, his feelings of lack, his need for God, and his desire to get involved in a church. I found it interesting that I never once mentioned anything to Coach about his salvation or about church. Simply by the example of my life and allowing myself to be the extension of God's hand of compassion, he automatically was drawn with a desire to know Jesus in an intimate way. We talked for quite a while; I shared with him how I was committed to helping him through this difficult time, and asked him if I could pray for him. I could see God's hope beginning to rise up on the inside of his heart.

As I got back in my car to head home, I was on fire! In those few moments with Coach, something had been ignited in my life that had been lying dormant for a long, long time. The thrill and passion of taking a risk, stepping off the cliff, and trusting God during the free fall had been painfully absent, and I knew that this was what had been missing from my life. The mediocrity I had been despising, and the dissatisfaction I had been wrestling with was all because I had forgotten why I entered into the ministry in the first place. I had gotten so busy with the business of helping people, that I had misplaced my genuine motive for people!

Now, all of a sudden, those questions about purpose, significance, legacy, and making a genuine, lasting difference became very clear. I prayed, "Lord, I want to do this for the rest of my life. I may never preach a crusade to thousands of people, have a worldwide ministry, or become a household name, but if you will give me the grace and the opportunities, I will do my best to serve humanity one person at a time for nothing more than the glory of God!" This was my first Second Mile experience, and it was like a drug. I was thoroughly addicted, and I desperately wanted more.

The Second Mile. It's a challenge. It's an invitation. It's a risk, but it's a thrilling adventure. It's in this kind of living we will find our true self, the self found in Christ. It's the laying down of what is comfortable, what is acceptable, and it's grabbing hold of a higher life...a life filled with a deeper satisfaction, precious personal sacrifice, and blessings beyond what we could ever have imagined in our wildest dreams.

The Second Mile. It's an appeal straight from the heart of God for you to revolutionize your world for Christ, to make a lasting impact that will resonate throughout eternity. The gun has sounded...the race has begun. Are you ready to go the distance? If so, let's get started!

CHAPTER TWO

Involvement

I played basketball for Louisiana College, a small school located in the heart of central Louisiana. The first time I visited the campus, I was on a recruiting trip with my father. As we drove over Red River and into the city limits of Pineville, we were met with an odor so powerful it was tangible. The best way to describe it is a combination of a wet dog, a dozen rotten eggs, and a junior high boys' locker room on a hot day. I looked over at my Dad and accused, "What is that terrible smell? Did you do that!?" After arguing with each other over who was responsible, we rolled down the windows and realized the aroma was definitely not coming from inside the car.

Not wanting to offend the college recruiters, I waited for an opportune time late in the day to inquire about the smell. We learned the town had a paper mill right across the street from the college, and they assured me that after about two weeks I would not even notice it. This was very hard for me to believe, but my passion to play basketball overrode my aversions for the odor, so I accepted the athletic scholarship. As strong as that paper mill smell could be, those recruiters were right. Over time, I did learn to live with it, and in fact, even reached the point of forgetting it was there.

The first time my wife came to visit the school, she and I were driving into the community, over the same Red River, and onto the campus. The smell hit Rachel like a ton of bricks. She looked at me, expecting to see a grimace, but only saw nonchalance; she took that to be a look of admission. "Oh Mike!" she groaned, "Was that you?!" Laughing, I told her not to worry—it was the pleasant paper mill next door. "Give it a little time," I said. "You'll get used to it." As those words spilled out of my mouth, I remembered my first day on campus and the incredible disbelief I felt at the recruiter's suggestion that there would ever come a day I would not notice that awful smell. How had my sense of smell become so tolerant and insensitive to something so blatantly unacceptable?

When I began my Christian walk as a teenager, I had incredible zeal and passion for the things of God. I remember looking at some of the 'older' Christians and judging them for not racing to get front row seats at every service, for not shooting up their hands at the first downbeat of praise and worship, and for not even bringing their Bibles or notebooks so they could take detailed notes during the sermon. I deemed them lazy Christians and vowed I would never allow myself to settle into that kind of mediocrity. It's funny how we think ourselves to be so wise at that age, and I certainly wore my cloak of omniscience with pride. If only I'd have had a snapshot of my future self, the self I described in the previous chapter who was full of the business of God, but empty of the passionate pursuit of God. If I would have been able to forecast how sneakily mediocrity was going to seep into my life, I would not have been so quick to judge those 'older' Christians around me. Just like the odor of that paper mill that at first was vile but over time became completely acceptable to me, so had mediocrity settled into my Christianity.

We live in a world full of shortcuts and a pervading attitude that says, "Do just enough to get by." Cutting corners is the name of the game in business. The norm in our culture is to live only for self and to avoid inconvenience at all costs. Our society is constantly finding new ways to celebrate the average, and as Christians, it is very easy to carry these habits into our walk with Christ. But as followers and imitators of Jesus, He has called us to an entirely different kind of living. If we attempt to live out our Christianity with the same selfish, compromising mind-set by which the world operates its affairs, we will inevitably end up feeling empty and dissatisfied. It is only when we decide to remove the comfortable blanket of mediocrity and to embrace this Second Mile way of life that the excitement and the adventure truly begin.

WHAT IF I DON'T?

Perhaps no other story in Scripture captures the essence of Second Mile living better than the story of the Good Samaritan. In Luke 10, Jesus explains what it means to "love your neighbor as yourself" by telling a story of a Jewish man who traveled from Jerusalem to Jericho. This fifteen-mile trek was a particularly dangerous one, littered with brigands and thieves, and few ever journeyed alone because of these safety risks. Sure enough, the man was attacked by bandits who beat him, robbed him, stripped him of his clothes, and left him for dead on the side of the road.

The first person to encounter the man in the ditch was a Jewish priest who was probably on his way to the synagogue. The priest should have been the principal person to stop, seeing this man was one of his own, possibly even a member of his own congregation. However, he seemed to be more interested in having church than being the church because he quickly crossed to the other side of the road. I am sure he was equipped with a beautifully eloquent, well-crafted sermon, but that was of little use to the man bleeding to death.

Sometimes I think we have a tendency to substitute Christian rhetoric for Christ-like compassion, and feel like we are really pleasing God. God is not interested in our clever little sayings or our pompous church lingo...and neither is a needy world. It's not our knowledge of scripture that makes us useful to God, but our willingness to put into

tion the things we have been taught. Scripture tells us, *"Whatever you have learned or received or heard from me, or seen in me—**put it into practice**. And the God of peace shall be with you."* (Philippians 4:9, NIV) Sad to say, many of us, like the priest, are educated far beyond our level of obedience. The broken and battered man did not need to hear a sensational sermon on the love of God—he needed to see one in action! By passing up the man in the ditch, the priest missed a golden opportunity to preach his most powerful message yet.

The second person to come onto the scene was a Levite, or a temple assistant. He walked over to the ditch and looked at the man in curiosity but thought, "Poor, misfortunate fella'. Wish I had time to help, but I've got too many things to do. Gotta' get to the temple or I'll be late!" He could not afford to be interrupted because his schedule was more important than someone else's pain. Rushing off to the temple, he thought he was keeping his appointment with God. Little did he know that God was lying there in the ditch—hidden in disguise.

I am convinced that Jesus is all around us just waiting to be discovered. He hides Himself in the homeless that walk our city streets. He looks like a widow who waits for a visit in a nursing home. He resembles an orphan that longs for a mom and dad. He is the next-door neighbor whose troubled teenager has just run away from home. The temple assistant hustled to the synagogue where, I am sure, he and the priest compared notes. But if they would have looked a bit deeper inside, beyond their excuses, beyond their 'duties,' I think they would have found a much more dominating motivation for their lack of involvement.

They were afraid...afraid of the bandits that committed this crime because certainly they were skulking about waiting for their next victim...afraid of what their constituents might think if they found out they had touched an 'unclean,' bloody man...afraid of what this act of compassion might involve. How much time will it take? How much money might I have to spend? If I stop to help this guy, then am I going to have to stop to help the next guy? The primary question circling around in their minds was: *What will happen to me if I get involved?*

Finally, a Samaritan man walks up and sees his Jewish counterpart in the ditch. The Jews and Samaritans had a long history of hate that rivaled the discrimination and segregation of our own recent American battles to establish civil rights. In spite of their cultural and religious differences, this Samaritan man did the unthinkable. He knelt beside the injured man, bandaged his wounds, put him on his own donkey, and brought him to the nearest inn for care. Unlike the first two men, the Good Samaritan did not let interruption or inconvenience keep him from stopping. The first two men stayed on the path—only one decided to go off-road and demonstrate the tangible, Second Mile love of God. The first two men were thinking, *What will happen to me if I get involved?* while the Samaritan was thinking quite the opposite, *What will happen to him if I don't get involved?*

> **I am convinced that Jesus is all around us just waiting to be discovered.**

Imagine where humanity would be today if Jesus Christ would have been sitting comfortably on His throne in heaven, One with God, possessing complete omniscience, omnipotence, and omnipresence, and when He looked down upon the lost and hopeless world, He thought, *What will happen to Me if I give all this up to save those sinful creatures?* It's absolutely unfathomable the kind of complete ruin we would be experiencing today. The only thought Jesus had resonating in His heart was, *What will happen to all these people if I don't get involved?!*

Jesus is the perfect picture of what Second Mile living is all about. He is the embodiment of selflessness, sacrifice, and serving. Aren't you glad that when you are beaten down by life and your own bad decisions have left you naked on the side of the road, Jesus doesn't pass by on the other side of your pain? In our most helpless moments, He always goes the Second Mile for us by getting into our ditch, putting us on His back, and carrying us to a place of healing. Romans 5:6-8 says, *"When we were utterly helpless, Christ came at just the right time and died for us sinners. Now, no one is likely to die for a good person, though someone might be willing to die for a person who is especially good. But God showed his great love for us by sending Christ to die for us while we were still sinners."* (NLT) When God looked down from heaven and saw us struggling in the ditch of our sins, He made a decision to get involved.

In Jesus' final moments on earth, He walked painstakingly up a hill with a cross on his back and literally went the Second Mile for you and for me. (Some Biblical experts say the road to Calvary—from Bethany to Jerusalem—is a two-mile hike.) Fighting through excruciating pain and fatigue, Jesus was on a mission to fulfill the will of His Father. He sacrificed His life for us by dying a criminal's death on a cross. By refusing to stop at mile one, He went the distance—becoming all that we are, so that one day we could become everything He is!

Did Jesus sacrifice so much, so that you and I could live so little? Are you living in the ordinary, or in God's realm of extra-ordinary? Today, too many of our churches are littered with decent Christians, but God is searching the earth to and fro looking for dangerous ones! He's desperate for men and women like us to leave our nice, cozy, predictable routines, to step outside of our own comfort zones, and to go the extra mile in order to reach into someone else's pain.

The apostle Paul understood how to live dangerously for Christ; he was the Braveheart, the Rambo, the Patriot of his day. He was ever trying to impart this mind-set into the lives of those who followed him. In 2 Corinthians 6:11-13 he writes: *"Dear, dear Corinthians, I can't tell you how much I long for you to enter this wide-open, spacious life. We didn't fence you in. The smallness you feel comes from within you. Your lives aren't small, but you're living them in a small way. I'm speaking as plainly as I can and with great affection. Open up your lives. Live openly and expansively!"* (The Message Bible) This passage captures the essence of Second Mile living. This is Christianity at its best: opening up our lives expansively, going beyond what is expected, and demonstrating a radical love for God and an irrational love for people.

There is no life comparable to the Second Mile life! As you read this book, you will be challenged to cover more ground in your faith than you ever thought possible. You will realize that Second Mile moments are not reserved for the spiritually elite. Ordinary people like you and me, who dare to look past ourselves and reach out in radical love to those around us, will come to know this higher living in which God has called us. Every day, we have opportunities to go the distance and express Second Mile love in practical ways. Mother Teresa once said, "People don't change the world with great deeds, but by small deeds done with great love." Let's go change our world!

EVERY LAP COUNTS

Just as a runner must carefully strategize each lap to qualify for the prize, so must we spend the time to study and to meditate upon the principles of God in order to hear Him proudly declare at the end of our life's journey: "Well done, My good and faithful servant." The Second Mile life is not simply about finishing, it is about stretching our chests forward to break the tape of our race...The Second Mile is about running to win.

SECTION ONE // LAP ONE

Getting Started

Everything in the kingdom of God is about growth and producing fruit. God expects us not only to be faithful but to be fruitful as well. In Matthew 25, Jesus tells a story that has become one of His most famous parables, The Parable of the Talents. It is about three servants each who were entrusted with different talents (sums of money) from their master. The first two servants took their talents and invested them, doubling what they originally had. The third servant took no risk, sought only to protect what was given to him, and buried the money in a nearby field.

After a period of time, the master returned to discover what progress his servants had made, and when he found the first two had doubled their sums, he blessed them. He said, "Well done, good and faithful servants!" and he gave them even more. When the third produced only the original sum, confessing he had done nothing to increase it, the master condemned him, calling him "wicked and lazy," and he took what he had given away from the servant and gave it to the first servant.

God has given each and every one of us gifts and talents to use for His Kingdom purposes, and He expects us to grow and to multiply them. So many times, we find ourselves requesting more from God, yet we have not even begun to do anything with what He already has given us. Why would He give us more? That's just bad investing!

What is interesting about this parable of the servants is the verdict pronounced to the third one. He is scolded not because he did something bad, but because he did nothing at all! I am convinced that had the servant at least tried diligently to produce increase, and even if he had lost every penny, God would have commended him on his attempts and blessed him like the others. God does not expect perfection, but He does demand progress! We've all been called to greatness…let's refuse to stay in the First Mile and go forward to the Second!

SECOND MILE STRETCHES:
1. What are your God-given gifts? Are you using them to their full capacity? Find some ways you can improve upon them.
2. Have you hidden any talents out of fear or insecurity? Be honest with yourself, and talk to a close friend or mentor about how you can begin to step out in faith and use these gifts. It's never too late to begin!
3. Be constantly on the lookout for new gifts. Remember, because of his faithfulness, God blessed the first servant with what He had originally given to the third.

NOTES:

SECTION ONE // LAP TWO

Preparation

"Study to show yourself approved unto God, a worker who does not need to be ashamed, rightly dividing the word of truth." (2 Tim. 2:15 NKJV)

I spend a lot of time with college age men and women, and sometimes after a service, students will come up for prayer asking me to agree with them that God will provide grace for their exams. Before praying, I always ask, "Have you studied and prepared for the test?" There are always those kids who give me a sheepish smile and confess their lack of diligence in reviewing the material. To these, I recommend a regime of Red Bull, plenty of snacks, and many hours of moonlight studying before I offer up some "God-bail-me-out-of-this" prayer!

We've all found ourselves in situations where we realize our less than desirable circumstances are only because of our lack of attention and preparation. And while God promises to always provide a way of escape, He does not guarantee that 'way of escape' will be easy...He also has set into motion the spiritual law of sowing and reaping! In addition, we can never rely on the anointing of the Holy Spirit to flow through us when we are completely unprepared (Read about Samson in the Book of Judges for this sobering reality). God will do His part only after we have done ours.

Just as an athlete has daily disciplines he must complete in order to be prepared for the big race, we must live every day filled with the strength and energy of the Holy Spirit, ready to engage in His plan for us! For every person and through different seasons of life, these disciplines can vary, but the diet is made up of the same ingredients: prayer time, study time, worship time, commitment to a local church, and the like. There is nothing more exciting than seeing God work through our lives on a daily basis, but this can only happen if we have prepared beforehand.

CONFESSION

Thank you, God, for helping me to remain diligent in my passionate pursuit of You every single day. Show me any areas I can improve my preparation to continue in the Second Mile life, and the ways by which to go to new levels. I will have eyes to see and ears to hear You as you prompt me with your Holy Spirit to bless those I come in to contact with today. Thank you for using me as your servant!

NOTES:

SECTION ONE // LAP THREE

Excellence

Excellence is a big deal to God. Repeatedly throughout the Bible, this is the word used to describe His presence, His works, and His nature. In fact, in the final book of the Old Testament, God has some harsh things to say to a group of priests who were practicing mediocrity. Under the Old Covenant, a sacrificial system was used as a covering for man's sin. Priests would offer an animal sacrifice—a goat, ram, sheep, or bull—and the shedding of that animal's blood would atone for the condition of man's sin. The law required that the animal be the best of the flock, without blemish, but these priests' sacrifices were unacceptable because they were giving less than their very best.

Malachi 1:8 *"When you give blind animals as sacrifices, isn't that wrong? And isn't it wrong to offer animals that are crippled and diseased?...I am not at all pleased with you," says the Lord Almighty, "and I will not accept your offerings."* (NLT)

Today, God does not require this Old Testament sacrificial system because Jesus Christ was made the perfect sacrifice. *"Once for all time He took blood into that Most Holy Place, but not the blood of goats and calves. He took His own blood, and with it He secured our salvation forever."* (Hebrews 9:12, NLT) But He does require us to walk out our Christianity with an attitude of excellence.

God gave us His absolute best, not some broken down angel, to solve our sin issue. He sent His only Son. He didn't have fifteen to choose from...He only had one. We must never diminish the significance of this sacrifice: The Darling of heaven, the sinless, spotless Lamb of God was crucified for our sin. When we truly come face to face with this reality of the Cross, we cannot remain mediocre. We are compelled to make a decision, nothing less than that which Paul spoke about in Romans 12:1. "Give your bodies to God. Let them be a living and holy sacrifice— the kind he will accept. When you think of what He has done for you, is this too much to ask?" (NLT) A life of excellence is the Second Mile Christianity that God is looking for.

CONFESSION

Today I will make a decision to go for excellence in every area of my life. God, your Spirit lives inside of me, and I thank You that you help me to recognize those areas where I have settled for second best. In Jesus' Name, give me the courage, the discipline, and the motivation to live this day as a Second Mile Christian.

NOTES:

SECTION ONE // LAP FOUR

Attitude

God cares about the details of our day and promises to be involved with our every step. However, even more than our activities and what we are doing, He is concerned about who we are becoming within our character. Colossians 3:23-24 says, "Work hard and cheerfully at whatever you do, as though you were working for the Lord rather than for people. Remember that the Lord will give you an inheritance as your reward, and the Master you are serving is Christ." (NLT)

For some of us, this oftentimes can become challenging because we are in job situations that are less than what we desire. Perhaps we have an over-demanding boss, or negative and apathetic co-workers, and we are losing motivation to get out of bed in the morning because we dread going to work and are struggling to find purpose in why we are there. Eventually, our performance will begin to slide because our attitude has soured.

We cannot always immediately change the circumstances we find ourselves in, but we can make a decision to change our attitude. Our earthly assignments have been given to us by God, and our lives are to be lived unto Him. Remember, He promises to fulfill the deepest desires of our hearts, and when we give our best effort in spite of our surroundings, God is pleased, and His purposes are being fulfilled. Before we know it, He will open the doors needed for each of us to walk into the jobs and careers we have always dreamed of. God will reward our commitment to excellence, and our destinies will be realized as we commit to attitudes of excellence in our small, daily, habitual routine.

SCRIPTURES TO MEDITATE ON:

Delight yourself in the Lord and He will give you the desires of your heart. (Psalm 37:4, NIV)

For I know the thoughts and plans I have for you, says the Lord, Plans for good and not evil so you will have peace and hope in your final outcome. (Jeremiah 29:1, NKJV)

NOTES:

SECTION ONE // LAP FIVE

Overcoming Fear

It's motivating to learn about the challenges of Second Mile Christianity, but many of us are afraid to take the risks involved because of fear. Fear of failure, fear of man, fear of fear! We think, "What if I try and fall flat on my face? What will other people think? What if I get criticized and questioned? What if I totally mess up and embarrass myself?" If we never get past these 'what if?' questions, we will never know what can be.

But 2 Timothy 1:7 promises: *God did not give us a spirit of timidity (of cowardice, of craven and cringing and fawning fear), but He has given us a spirit of power and of love and of a calm and well-balanced mind and discipline and control. (AMP)*

The process works like this: If we try, we may fail. But we learn, and then we grow. So we can try again! It's pretty simple—kind of kindergarten cut-and-paste. You may take a risk and absolutely blow it...so what! Welcome to the human race, a collective group of people who are expert at getting it wrong. Our desire for perfection is in reality bondage because in our attempt to avoid imperfection we don't attempt anything at all.

The truth is, we need our mistakes. That is how children learn to do just about anything: walk, swim, ride bikes, hit a baseball, or do a cartwheel. None of these skills can be mastered without a few bumps and bruises along the way, but the joys they bring far outweigh the pain of the process. The same is true in our journey with Christ. As we learn and grow we are sure to make mistakes, but the rewards of our faithfulness will always be greater than the sacrifices. At the end of your life, you will not regret the risks you took, only the ones you were never brave enough to embrace.

God takes us just as we are—flawed, fearful, and full of mistakes—and uses us as agents of healing in a desperately hurting world. Second Mile living is not reserved for perfect people; it's available to ordinary people like you and me who long to be used by God to make a difference. If we give God what we have, He will give us everything we need to accomplish all He has called us to do.

SECOND MILE MINDSETS:

1. If I am feeling fear about stepping out in a particular area…I do it anyway.
2. I am not concerned about what man thinks of me if I step out; I am way more concerned about what God will think of me if I don't.
3. If at first I don't succeed, try and try again!

NOTES:

SECTION TWO:
upward

Our quest for the Second Mile life begins with our relationship with God. As we worship Him with our very lives, with the depth of our beings, we find our true selves. Doubts are dispelled, dreams are discovered, and true love emerges. As deep calls unto deep between our spirits and His, a life beyond our imagination will begin to manifest.

CHAPTER THREE

Passion for God

There is a strange epidemic that rapidly spreads across Southern Louisiana every autumn; it's highly contagious, it indiscriminately infects men, women, and children alike, and even with our advances in medicine, a cure is still unknown. Symptoms include elevated heart rates, spontaneous spastic physical behavior, loss of vocal abilities due to frequent, sudden eruptions, and in some very severe cases, a man's skin on his face, neck and chest can turn purple and golden yellow. Thousands upon thousands fall victim each year to this erratic condition, and the only thing we do know about this phenomena is that the source of its contamination comes from Louisiana State University. It is called: Tiger Fever!

Every game day at LSU, over 90,000 fans lucky enough to get a ticket, pack inside the football stadium ready to raise the roof for their beloved Tigers. These frenzied fans are completely decked out in LSU garb, detailed with the Tiger hat, the big foam finger, and a cowbell ready to sound...God help the poor soul who accidentally wore the opposing team's colors...we may never see him again. Tiger Stadium is electrifying on these Saturday nights as ordinary men and women turn into something other-wordly as they cheer their Tigers on to victory. They are unashamed. They are passionate. They have Tiger Fever!

I have to admit, I've always been a basketball guy; it's my sport of preference, and is what I played throughout college. But once inside that stadium, as the energy from the other 90,000 fans begins to sweep through like a heavy current, I find myself standing to my feet screaming like a Banshee, looking for someone with some extra purple face paint so I can graffiti my face. It's amazing to see what an entire community can create, and one thing is certain: passion is contagious.

Every single one of us is a creature of passion. Even those of us who consider ourselves quiet and refined, if a person starts to poke around in our hearts, asking questions that might challenge a core belief or something we truly care about...stand back and watch the passion arise! We are created in the likeness and image of God Himself, so truly, we cannot be anything other than a passionate being.

Passion is a powerful force as well as a crucial element to the Second Mile life. An unashamed and unrelenting passion for Jesus and for His desires ignites our hearts and gives us the long-term fuel required to offer our lives for the service of His people. Without this deep-seated passion for God, most Christians will never make it past the first mile. Although we start our Christian walk fervently and ready to charge hell with a water pistol, as soon as it gets difficult (which it always does) or as soon as we face opposition (which we always will), we find ourselves out of breath. Not wanting to feel too uncomfortable, not wanting to rock the proverbial boat too much, we decide to slow down and to look for a more 'reasonable' Christianity.

> **Passion is a powerful force as well as a crucial element to the Second Mile life.**

Often during our almost ten years of serving as youth pastors, Rachel and I saw this pattern in the young people. It was very exciting for us to see them get serious about their relationships with Christ and to watch as they fully surrendered their lives to worship Him. They had no concerns about what anyone else thought of them; they were too busy imagining how they, with the help of the Holy Spirit, were going to change the world. Their dreams and desires reflected the size of their faith in the God of the Impossible.

Then as some grew older, graduating from high school and entering college, things began to change. Their red-hot passion for God seemed to cool off. They were no longer brimming with life on the front row of our worship services. They seemed to drift into a casual, been-there-done-that, I'm-all-grown-up-now mentality. Somehow, the idea was that passion and maturity were now incompatible. They, like many of us, bumped up against the lie that says because of marriage, career, a mortgage, children, and bills we need to 'grow out' of that immature passionate behavior and to float along a current of something mellow, boring, and passive…something more 'acceptable' and 'reasonable.'

'Acceptable' and 'reasonable' are the last adjectives that would be used to describe Jesus. He was passionate! He was dangerous! And He is our example, not whatever social norms happen to be popular in our culture. In the Gospel of John, Chapter 2, the Bible paints a picture of just how passionate Jesus was for God and the things of God.

On this particular day, Jesus walked into the temple and saw both the moneychangers and the merchants operating their businesses without integrity. First, because people traveled from many different nations to come to offer their sacrifices in Jerusalem, they were required to exchange their native currency in order to purchase what they needed. The moneychangers were offering only extremely inflated rates. Second, the merchants who bought and sold the items necessary for the Jewish people to offer their sacrifices were also unfairly charging their customers.

Jesus became furious at these business people who were using what was supposed to be sacred as a vehicle to satisfy their greed and dishonest personal gain. Scripture tells us that Jesus made a whip and single-handedly—in one fell 'Indiana Jones' swoop—turned over their tables, scattered their money, and ran them out of the sanctuary! Now that's passion. In fact, the following verses record the disciples remembering a prophetic scripture from the book of Psalms that says, "Passion for God's house burns within me." At that moment, they knew they were seeing this scripture fulfilled.

Now, some might interpret this kind of passion as rash, reckless, and even out of control. But a careful read reveals this: Jesus encountered the offense, and then went away and made a whip. I'm not a whip-making expert, but I know it had to take a few hours to gather the supplies, cut the leather properly, braid the pieces together, and attach them securely to the handle. Not to mention, the time required to brush up on His whip wielding accuracy; after all, no one was hurt during His conquest. No, this kind of passion was focused, intentional, and motivated by a pure heart driven to protect the integrity of His Father's house. He made no excuses, nor did He care what others might think of Him, for He was a man filled with a heart of passion for God.

This passion caused Jesus to become a powerful magnet for masses of people. Everyone who encountered Christ felt the pulse of His passion for truth and righteousness and they recognized there was something radically different in Him, a quality that was definitely missing in their own lives. Simply by His example, He would put people in touch with the nature and intensity of the deep emptiness they had in their spirits and souls. For the first time, many began to see how unfulfilled their lives were, how thirsty their choices had left them, and as a result, their eyes were opened to The Way of Salvation. Jesus inspired them to a higher level of living...a Second Mile life.

The Second Mile life requires this kind of passion. It's not hype or a changeable emotion; it's an issue of the heart. It's fueled and sustained from within, from a vibrant and consistent relationship with Jesus. You won't be able to find passion in a pill or a bottle. You cannot order it off E-bay, the Home Shopping Network, or even a Billy Maze infomercial.

It's a fire in your belly ignited by God Himself when you make a quality decision to give yourself unconditionally to His plan and His purpose, and it's sustained by a daily pursuit of our Father's heart.

A life of passion will always engage the interest of others. When we begin to live our lives in a passionate, purposeful way, we will become powerful magnets to whom others are drawn. If God is the Source of passion, and you and I are plugged into the Source, shouldn't we reflect this quality? Shouldn't passion be the common quality that distinguishes all of God's people from the rest of the world? Let's stir up our passion for God!

PURSUING GOD'S PASSION

When Rachel and I were dating, we spent many, many hours at the mall. I would call her after work and ask her what she wanted to do, and nine times out of ten, she would say, "Let's go to the mall!" My response was the same, "Baby, I was hoping you would say that. I've been thinking about the mall all day long! Let's go and spend lots of money to get you the things you want!" It was easy to say that then because she was still spending her daddy's money, not mine! She loved shopping—I loved her—so I loved shopping...it was that simple. Her passions became my passions. It did not matter that my life pre-Rachel rarely found me inside a mall to simply 'look around.'

I'm a hunter and gatherer. Give me a mission to find a particular item so I can track it down, find the best one, purchase and bag it, and be back in the car in ten minutes flat. I used to secretly roll my eyes at those pitiful guys sitting on the sofas outside the women's fitting rooms. *Have they lost all sense of their manhood?* I used to think...until I became one of them. Dazzled by the true love of a beautiful woman, all bets were off, and there I would sit alongside the other boyfriends patiently waiting to lavishly compliment my girlfriend once she came out to model her new dress.

Four years of dating, over a decade of marriage, and three children later, I don't make it to the mall very much anymore. You certainly won't find me sitting for hours on one of those fitting room sofas. I would rather be doing something of global importance—something that will impact generations forever...like watching a football game! Now that's a real reason to rest one's body for hours upon a sofa! In fact, when I do have to go shopping, it is a grueling test of endurance. I'm like the old men who sit on the benches outside the stores and wait for their wives to come out. My passion has been reduced to obligation.

Passion can easily turn into obligation, without any warning signs, and it can infect a marriage, a career, and most destructively, our pursuit for God. Just like my shopping sprees with my wife, what was once done easily out of fervor to please the one that we love can become a chore after the newness of the romance wears off. We must never allow our Christianity to settle in to a cozy routine because then we will lose sight of what stirs God's passion—the lost and the hurting people in our world. And we will become blind to the opportunities to step outside of our own contentment in order to reach into someone else's pain.

> **Playing it safe will never produce God's best in you.**

Many of our churches today are full of decent Christians, who do all that is expected from them: they go to church every week, they smile and greet the new people, they tithe, they may even raise a hand or two momentarily in praise and worship, and then they go home to their ordinary lives. I certainly am not trying to discount their efforts or their faith in Jesus, but there is so much more available for them! These Christians have allowed their passions to turn into obligation, and they have settled into a Christianity that never goes beyond the First Mile.

Playing it safe will never produce God's best in you. You were born for something far, far greater. History shows that men and women who have impacted their generations for the glory of God did so by pushing the boundaries of what others thought to be safe and trusting themselves to God alone. This is Christianity at its best: going beyond what is expected to demonstrate a radical love for God and an irrational love for people. This is the essence of the Second Mile life, and passion is the fuel that enables us to sustain it.

Everything Jesus ever did, He did it in a passionate way. When He worked, He worked with passion. When He gave, He gave with passion. When He healed, He healed with passion. When He taught, He taught with passion. When He loved, He loved with passion. When He cried, He was moved with passion. And when He died, Jesus died with passion! In fact, even the world's wisdom acknowledges and equates Jesus with passion; any dictionary lists as one of its definitions for passion: "the suffering and death of Jesus."

As we daily ignite our fervor for God, His passions will become our passions. This pursuit will undoubtedly result in an unquenchable desire to care for people—all kinds of people. Black, white, rich, poor, educated, uneducated, lovely, unlovely, religious, non-religious—all people matter to God. We will find ourselves loving people enough to risk our own safety and our own reputation, just like God has done from the beginning of time and Jesus did every moment He walked upon the face of this earth. John 3:16 says, *"For God so loved the world that He gave His only Son, so that everyone who believes in Him will not perish but have eternal life." (NLT)* Now, that's some serious passion!

CHAPTER FOUR

Worship for God

I wonder if any of the adults in our neighborhood think I'm some sort of a Pied Piper? Many of the kids love to play the game hide-and-seek, and when I come home from work, as soon as they get a glimpse of my car pulling in our driveway, they come running. They literally swarm my parked car, yelling my name in a cacophony of cute voices, begging me to be 'it' in the next round of their childhood game. After a moment of reluctance (as I smell the amazing dinner my wife has prepared wafting from my house), I agree to play one game, and with excited shrills high enough to cause dogs to bark for miles, they scramble to their hiding places. The funny thing is, each one of them always hides in the exact same spot!

In order to make the game last longer than three minutes, I begin my hunt pretending to have no idea in the world where each one of them could be. Believing my ignorance, the kids begin to make little sounds and giggles so they can signal me toward their amazingly clever secret hideouts. They bubble with excitement because they cannot wait to be found, and the excitement of the pursuit culminates in the joy of discovery!

It is important to know that God is on the lookout too. The Bible says that God is searching for an authentic group of people who will set their hearts to worship Him. John 4:23 says: *"The time is coming and is already here when true worshipers will worship the Father in spirit and in truth. The Father is looking for anyone who will worship him that way." (NLT)* If God is looking for true worshipers, then that tells me there must be other kinds of worshipers out there. People of the Second Mile are committed to seeking God with purity and integrity in their worship, and when we worship Him in that manner, we become exactly what God is searching for. If God is on the lookout, I want Him to find me.

In much the same way as these kids' vocal cues to me, our worship signals heaven and gives God our exact location. It's almost like sending a flare up into the sky and announcing, "Here I am God! Look over here!" Now God is not in heaven, confused and scratching His head wondering where you are. He knows your exact address, your name, your history, your achievements, your heartache, and your concerns. But your sincere worship grabs His attention. It not only causes you to shift your focus from an earthly perspective to a spiritual one, it also invites His presence and enlists His help into every situation.

> **In its simplest form, worship is love responding to love.**

Normally, when we talk about worship, our discussions stay confined to churchy scenarios of music and instruments, of choirs swaying amidst a sea of satiny robes, maybe even an organ piping from a balcony. At the small church where I grew up, we used to sing out of the hymnal *(I always wondered why we would sing the first, second, and fourth verses. What was wrong with verse three?)*. Worship is so much more than a fifteen or twenty minute Sunday morning routine, so far beyond a song from our lips. Second Mile worship is the music of our lives. Our entire existence should be a constant expression of worship and devotion to Jesus.

There are probably many different deep, theological ideas of what worship is, but in its simplest form, worship is love responding to love.

It is our love responding to God's love, our actions replying to the God who every moment in history has given us nothing but His very best. I John 4:10 says, *"But this is real love, not that we loved God but that He first loved us, and sent His Son as a sacrifice to take away our sins."* (NLT) Jesus offered up the supreme sacrifice so that we might have an abundant life, and this should demand from us nothing less than complete honor and utter devotion. That is so much more than a Sunday musical experience! You and I do not have much to offer back to God; every gift, every opportunity, every good thing we possess has been given to us by Him. The only thing we can truly present Him in return is our choice to worship Him with every aspect of our lives.

The book that has impacted my life more than any other—outside of the Bible—is called *The Practice of the Presence of God.* This work, a collection of documented conversations and letters from a man commonly referred to as Brother Lawrence, has turned my life inside out. Brother Lawrence was a short-order cook and a dishwasher at a French monastery during the 17th century, and his relationship with the Lord was so alive he was able to turn even the most menial task into a living hymn to the glory of God. He wrote, "The time of business does not with me differ from the time of prayer, and in the noise and clatter of my kitchen...I possess God in as great tranquility as if I were upon my knees at the Blessed Sacrament."

What a truly awesome thought! We can worship God anywhere, anytime; with just a thought or a word, we can instantly be in fellowship with Him. As a child of the Most High God, we have a private audience with the King of Kings, a sanctuary with the Creator of the Universe. He makes Himself available to us throughout the day, even desperately desires this kind of fellowship with us. Everyone is capable of this kind of "habitual, silent, and secret conversation of the soul with God." In James 4, the writer reminds us that God is a jealous God, desiring our full attention, and when we draw close to Him, He is ever faithful to draw close to us. God yearns to be a part of every aspect of our lives and is just as concerned with our ordinary, day-to-day responsibilities as He is with our spiritual experiences.

The problem is we opt Him out of our mundane moments of life because we think He's not really interested in such 'normal' tasks. We compartmentalize our lives into what is sacred and what is secular, inviting God to have His way in the spiritual and leaving Him out of the rest. We have a very confused scoring system that values church and ministry activities as a '10' and the chores of work and family as '4' or '5.' What we must come to understand is God rates everything as a '10.'

> **It is in the daily, ordinary tasks where our true worship begins.**

In my early years of ministry, I felt like my days were filled with the exciting labor of building our youth ministry, and I would come home feeling very energized and proud of the work I was doing. I deemed myself a regular Bible superhero…until my wife would ask me to mow the grass, or change our baby's stinky diaper. I can remember sensing a bit of indignation inside, thinking, *Does this woman not know whom she is asking to perform these mundane, earthly tasks? Is she not aware of my superhuman alter ego?* I considered these tasks to be far less sacred than the ones I was occupied with as I was about 'my Father's business.' I could not have been more wrong.

As I studied the life of Brother Lawrence, the Holy Spirit helped me to correct my thinking and understand that actually, it is in the daily, ordinary tasks where our true worship begins. So many of us compartmentalize 'worship' into a stained glass Sunday experience, and use this time to accept refreshment, healing and fellowship from our Father. It's more about what we can receive from Him as we dutifully throw in a few 'thank you's' and 'you're so holy's.' This is what I would describe as First Mile worship. But just by looking at the life of Jesus we can realize there is so much more to worship! Every moment, His life of worship was entrenched in service for all people, to the utmost of giving His body to be crucified and His spirit into the depths of despair. Christ's worship was extremely generous and selfless; His worship exemplifies Second Mile worship. When we give ourselves fully to this model of sacrifice, we will discover a lifestyle of worship more fulfilling, more exciting, more dynamic than we've ever imagined.

COMPLETELY HIS

"Love the Lord your God with all your heart and with all your soul and with all your mind." (Matthew 22:37, NIV)

Jesus said to love God with all our being. After doing some extensive research in Greek and Aramaic, I found that the word "all" in any language literally means, ALL —not some, or even most, but all. We are to give Him everything: our lives, our thoughts, our achievements, our failures, our fears...everything. For many of us, this is the sole obstacle that keeps us from possessing the life of a *true* worshipper. We have one foot in the church, and the other in the world. We love God enough to attend church on Sundays (well, almost every Sunday), but not enough to fellowship with His Son every single day. We struggle to walk in victory because our hearts are so divided. We are pulled in different directions, and it is almost like a tug-of-war; the lust of this world pulls us one way and the call of God's Spirit pulls us another. We find ourselves going through life like a wishbone, in constant tension being pulled by opposite forces. When we are caught in the middle, how do we decide which way to lean? Most of the time, it simply depends on how we are feeling at that particular moment...usually the worst determining factor.

We cannot truly worship God with a divided heart. Eventually, our double-mindedness will be exposed. The psalmist David wrote,

"Search me, O God, and know my heart. Try me and know my thoughts. See if there be any wicked way in me and lead me in the way everlasting." (Psalm 139:23-24) God is not satisfied with partial commitment or shallow interest; He wants ALL, and He certainly deserves nothing less. God is not some hobby that we recreationally entertain. He is not some spare tire that we only pull out in emergencies. He is the Creator of everything and the Lover of our eternal souls, and He alone holds the blueprints for what our lives should look like.

When we set our minds toward God and surrender ourselves to His goodness, the residue of this chaotic world is washed away from us. Then a beautiful thing happens; with clarity of vision, we can see who we really are in Christ, what the 'God' desires are deep in our hearts, and what we are truly called to do with our lives. Our perspective is shaped by heaven, and our actions are directed by the Spirit. We find we can praise God even in the midst of difficult and uncomfortable challenges. Although our circumstances may not change overnight, we understand God is much more interested in changing us than He is in changing our circumstances. What happens in us is always more important than what happens *around* us.

However, God cannot build on something He does not fully own. If you have ever lived in an apartment, you understand this principle completely. Those who rent are not allowed to make many improvements to their homes without the permission of the owners. But if you own your own home, your name is on the title. You know the joys of going to Lowe's or Home Depot for those house projects: building a deck, putting up a fence, or even adding a room. Any revisions are totally at your discretion (or should I say more specifically, the wife's discretion).

God is not looking for a room in our hearts to rent—He wants to own the whole house! If you and I belong to God, then the title to our entire lives has been deeded to Him. When we lease even a small portion of our hearts to other things, we treat God as some tenant who can be easily evicted. But when God makes His home in you, the possibilities of what you can be are limitless. He does not need your permission to do a single thing because you have trustfully signed over the title of your life to Him. He owes you no explanation and should never have to ask for your opinion or approval. You are His, completely! You merely offer yourself as raw material, willing to be cut, sanded, hammered, and shaped by the Master Carpenter for His use and His Kingdom purposes.

In His presence, as we worship Him with our lives, we begin a very important journey of discovery. Our lives are packed with so many different layers of experiences, emotions, feelings, and mindsets that we can, in fact, bury valuable information and become unaware of the content of our own soul. If we are oblivious to what is inside of us, then we will be powerless of what will come out of us. Worship allows us to excavate and unearth our personal history and to discover who we really are. In Psalm 16:11, David

> **God is not looking for a room in our hearts to rent—He wants to own the whole house!**

speaks to God saying, *"You will show me the path of life; In Your presence there is fullness of joy; At Your right hand are pleasures forevermore."* (NKJV) Our daily fellowship with Him makes us keenly aware of His perfectly ordered steps for us as He leads us along a path of abundant life. We learn about ourselves, and we are filled with the incredible joy of coming to intimately know God as well. What a tremendous, indescribable privilege.

POWER FOR THE SECOND MILE

There is an incredible amount of power available to each and every one of us when we make the choice to give our lives as a sacrifice of praise and worship. There has been no synthetic invention, no steroid, no amphetamine made available to humanity that is remotely comparable to the dynamic inner strength we can possess when we are plugged in to the circuit of the Almighty God. And for anyone who decides to embrace the Second Mile life, this power is not only extremely beneficial, it is a nonnegotiable! There is an amazing account in the Book of Acts about two such Second Milers who knew how to access this power.

In Acts 16, the apostle Paul and his partner, Silas, were blazing a trail for Jesus Christ and stirred up some fierce opposition in the city of Philippi. Their advance of the Gospel landed them a night in jail, only after a severe beating at the hands of an angry mob. Scripture tells us they were thrown into the inner dungeon and shackled with stocks around their feet. Now I don't know about you, but if I had just been beaten to a bloody pulp, stuck in a dark, vile cell and bound in chains, I'd begin to have some doubts about whether or not I should have given up my day job to become an evangelist. Not Paul and Silas...

The pivotal point of this story is found in Paul and Silas' astonishing response to their adversity. The Bible tells us, *"Around midnight, Paul and Silas were praying and singing hymns to God, and the other prisoners were listening. Suddenly, there was a great earthquake, and the prison was shaken to its foundations. All the doors flew open, and the chains of every prisoner fell off!"* (Acts 16:25-26, NLT) The outcome of their midnight worship was totally supernatural. God did for them what they could not do for themselves...He set them free! But notice how they praised *before* they were delivered. It is one thing to sing and shout *after* the miracle has already taken place, but quite another to do it when there is not even a hint that God is near.

This is what Second Mile worship is all about—praising Him even when you don't see the miracle or feel His presence. Paul and Silas were in terrible surroundings, but they didn't let their surroundings determine their song. Paul said, "If I can't sleep, the devil is not going to be able to sleep either! I am going to trumpet the praises of God!" What a perfect example for us to follow. Our praise and worship of God should be independent of our feelings and our circumstances; no matter what comes our way, we put our trust in Him and begin to praise Him simply for who He is. Inevitably, His presence and His power will make itself known, and before we know it, we are on our way to victory.

Praise plows through the days when nothing seems to go right—when the car breaks down, when the baby is up all night, when the check comes back NSF, when traffic makes you late for work again. Many times, we are just one praise away from a breakthrough. If we will climb the mountain with praise in our mouths, we will reach our miracle on the other side! If we look in the right places, we can always find plenty for which to be thankful. Sadly, we can get stalled in criticism and complaints and become blind to God's help that is just within reach. As a result, we never experience the victory that awaits us on the other side. Whining and complaining about how bad life is will only take us in circles. We will find ourselves going around the same mountains again and again. If we want a change of scenery, we need to sing a new song!

Sometimes, you might find yourself in a situation where you are lacking and are not finding the spiritual fortitude to muster up this kind of worship on your own. Not to worry...have the courage to call a friend to help. You see, the enemy messed up—not when he had them arrested, not when he had them beaten, not when he had them chained, but when he had Paul and Silas confined to the same cell *together*. He underestimated the dynamic power of agreement. Jesus had already said, *"For where two or three come together in my name, there am I with them."* (Matthew 18:20, NIV) They were confined, but they were together...and Jesus was right in the middle.

I believe the prison doors flew open, not because they were trying to break out, but because God was trying to break in!! God was looking to inhabit the praises of Paul and Silas and set them free—but not just them, everyone in the prison as well! Your steadfast worship of God, even in the middle of hostile circumstances, has the potential of breaking bondages off those around you—people in your family, people that you work with, those within your circle of influence. Praise and worship has a multiplied domino effect that can break the chains in your own life and release captives all around you.

If you are going through a crisis today, just remember that your battle cry is your praise and worship. King David was a worshiper before he was a warrior, before he became the greatest earthly king ever known to man. He learned the presence of God in the sheep field before he ever charged onto the battlefield. His worship was his launching pad to greatness. Before he ever started killing giants and conquering kingdoms, he learned the presence of God in the hidden valleys of faithfulness. He penned the words, *"I will bless the Lord at all times; His praise will continually be in my mouth."* (Psalm 34:1, NKJV) We must fill our mouths with praise if we want to be prepared to face our Goliaths. Only then will we be guaranteed His presence and His victory in the fight.

Be a Second Mile worshiper. Love God with all your heart, with all your soul, and with all your mind. Decide to be the one who will praise Him for all He has done and all He will do, no matter what your day looks like today. Jesus passionately loves you and wants to be involved with you, even the tiniest details of your life. As you operate in this strength and power, you will not only encounter blessings and victory in your life, you will also function in a freedom as never before. But most of all, you will experience the deep fulfillment of being used by God to bring liberty to those around you in ways you never dreamed possible.

EVERY LAP COUNTS

SECTION TWO // LAP ONE

God's Poem

When a poet constructs a piece of literature, he meditates upon every detail of that work. He visualizes the form, expresses himself by carefully selecting each and every word, and he does not finish until he believes his creation to be perfect. Did you know you were a poem of God? Ephesians 2:10 reads: *"For we are God's workmanship, created in Christ Jesus, to do good works which God prepared in advance for us to do."* (NIV) In the original Greek text, the word 'workmanship' is translated from the Greek word 'poiema,' meaning poem. Every part of you, the Master meticulously crafted so that He could express Himself through you in this world, at this time.

As God's work of art, we can never buy into the lie that we were created for anything less than extra-ordinary. We must be confident in the gifts He has given us and pursue to use them to their greatest capacity. Here on earth, the Church is the embodiment of the Almighty God, the visible expression of the heart and mind of God...we must never forget that! It is a tremendous responsibility every single Christian must own if we are going to be used to bring the message of salvation to all the nations.

And for those who might be feeling a bit of pressure right now... here's the good news: God prepared ahead of time the good works He planned for each of us to walk in! Just as He created our beings with great care, He fashioned each day for us before we were ever born, and we simply need to choose to obey His daily directions for those works. And if we get off course (which we are really great at doing), all we need is to repent and allow Him to redirect us into His perfect plan. It's not rocket science…He's not trying to trick us. God desires each of us to succeed in our Christian lives even more than we do because He needs us in order for His expression to be shown throughout the earth.

SCRIPTURES TO MEDITATE ON:

Psalm 139:14-16 For you created my inmost being; you knit me together in my mother's womb. I praise you because I am fearfully and wonderfully made; your works are wonderful, I know that full well. My frame was not hidden from you when I was made in the secret place. When I was woven together in the depths of the earth, your eyes saw my unformed body. All the days ordained for me were written in your book before one of them came to be. (NIV)

Psalm 37:23 The steps of a good man are ordered by the Lord, And He delights in his way. (NKJV)

NOTES:

SECTION TWO // LAP TWO

God's Word

Second Mile Christians are passionate about God's Word! In John 8:31-32 it says: To the Jews who had believed him, Jesus said, *"If you hold to my teaching you are really my disciples. Then you will know the truth, and the truth will set you free."* (NIV) This is such a powerful statement on many levels. First, Jesus only gave this nugget of Truth to the Jews who believed in Him, to those who had committed their hearts and their time to Him. Second, He teaches them they will only know the truth if they hold to His teachings, and incorporate them into their lives. Only then, will they come to understand the truth, and it is only those truths they understand that will set them free. So many Christians love the 'setting free' part, but they do not want to spend the time with the 'holding to My teaching' part.

If you were to take a ride with me in my faded silver, '99, Honda Accord LX, you would immediately notice several things. The back seat would resemble something like kinder-care for kids. I am fully equipped with disassembled Happy Meal toys, car seats, loose crayons, Coke stains, and scattered Skittles frequently left for spur-of-the-moment snacks. As a parent of three, that's how we travel. But before you could even sit down in the passenger seat, you would have to clear out stacks and cases of teaching tapes and CD's. Since I spend a lot of time in my car, I have decided to transform it into a mobile learning unit—when it's not a daycare on wheels.

I love to hear great preaching and teaching of God's Word. It compels me to a higher level of living and keeps me tuned in to the frequency of heaven. Sometimes when I am driving and God begins to speak to me through a tape or CD, I get out my little notepad and pen and start writing. This takes great skill and even greater faith because my car is a 5-speed and I have to write in between shifting gears!! (Caution: do not try this at home unless you plan on taking a shortcut to heaven.) But it is this passion for God's Word that has anchored me with hope in times of crisis, has hedged me in and protected me in times of potential danger, and has molded me into the husband, father, and minister I am today.

Second Mile Christians must have an insatiable hunger and thirst for the Word of God. If you are in a place where you have become complacent or lackadaisical for the study of The Truth, ask the Holy Spirit to rekindle this passion inside your heart. Then, act on your prayer and begin to make the time to soak your mind, heart, and soul in the refreshing and invigorating power of God's Word.

PRAYER

Father, thank you for Your Word that never changes, that is alive and powerful, and that alone has the power to save my soul. Holy Spirit, help me to stir up the passion within my heart for the study of the Word. Thank you for revealing to me deeper truths and teaching me about my daily life through the Word as I am faithful to study and to meditate on The Truth.

NOTES:

SECTION TWO // LAP THREE

God's Peace

An umpire in a baseball game is responsible for determining the legitimacy of every single pitch. He decides if the pitch is a strike or a ball, if the hit is fair or foul, or the runner into home plate is safe or out. No matter what the players, managers or coaches might think, no matter how the play in question appeared to everyone else, the umpire has the final authority. Arguing with his judgment only leads to being thrown out of the game.

Ephesians 3:15 says: *"For Whom every family in heaven and on earth is named [that Father from Whom all fatherhood takes its title and derives its name]." (AMP)* This peace of God, available to every Christian, must be our final authority for every decision as we navigate through the uncertainties of life. Some situations seem impossible to solve but God's peace within our heart can offer the answers. Some opportunities appear perfectly ordained, but God's peace will reveal what is true and what is merely distraction. Some challenges present paths that all seem difficult and wrong, but even in these, God's peace will light the correct path.

With the vast array of choices, conflicts, questions, and doubts we are confronted with, this reality should bring great comfort to our hearts. We are never alone, and when we learn to operate in God's peace, He is able to direct us not only with life-altering situations, but also in the minutia of our daily schedules. All it takes is a keen spiritual awareness to discern which way the Umpire of Peace is calling us...and therein lies the rub.

It takes a Second Miler to be able to function in this peace because we cannot hear God's voice when we are stressed out, negative, and saturated with the influence of the world. It takes practice tuning the spiritual ear into this still, small voice, and it takes the disciplining of our flesh to be quiet when obstacles or challenges arise. (Our flesh is always ready to boldly offer up its opinions, isn't it?) We must become sensitive to the direction of God's peace...He always knows what is best, He is the final authority, and arguing with His judgment only leads to being thrown out of the game.

SECOND MILE STRETCHES:

1. Take time each day to be quiet, to listen to God, and to practice being at peace. Learn how it feels to be at peace within your mind and heart, and strive to have this be your 'norm.'
2. Turn down your intake of the world news! Our media is designed to stir up negativity, conflict, and liberalism...all enemies of peace. Know the basics of what's happening in the world and leave it at that.
3. What kind of music and television shows are you watching? Do they foster a spirit of peace in your heart, or a spirit of fear, anxiety, doubt and worry?
4. If you are at a crossroads and do not know which way to go, don't simply stand there...make a choice and start walking. Keep an inward ear, and God will let you know right away if the path you chose was the right one.

NOTES:

SECTION TWO // LAP FOUR

God's Power

"He performs wonders that cannot be fathomed, miracles that cannot be counted." Job 5:9 (NIV)

This journey of going the Second Mile is not merely philanthropy, social justice, or good works; this is a spiritual quest. There is faith involved, impossibilities believed for, and God's supernatural power required. It's not simply the physical task of carrying something an extra mile; it is all about what is ignited spiritually as a result of that action. However, before God can get involved with His amazing power, we must be the catalyst by stepping out in faith with a natural action.

In Matthew 14, Jesus gave Peter an invitation to walk on the water. Peter's response needed to be something natural: get out of the boat and jump onto the sea. It wasn't until the moment Peter stepped out in faith by putting his feet into the water that the supernatural showed up and he was able to accomplish something that was impossible. Jesus is giving each one of us an invitation to do something impossible in our own strength, so supernatural that only God can be praised for such an achievement. We must take the first step and when we do our part, we can trust in God to do His.

God is able, and when we dare to believe in the supernatural enough to forget doubts and fear, we will be able to step into a life that is filled with His power to do the impossible. We will see miracles in our families, in our businesses, and in our everyday lives, and the result will be the lost believing in Christ and eternal lives being formed. Decide today to take on a miracle mindset and begin to look for opportunities to operate in God's power in every area of your life.

SCRIPTURES TO MEDITATE ON:

John 14:12 "The truth is, anyone who believes in me will do the same works I have done, and even greater works, because I am going to be with the Father." (NIV)

Mark 10:27 "Jesus looked at them and said, 'With man this is impossible, but not with God; all things are possible." (NIV)

Ephesians 3:20 "Now glory be to God! By his mighty power at work within us, he is able to accomplish infinitely more than we would ever dare to ask or hope." (NLT)

NOTES:

SECTION TWO // LAP FIVE

God's Joy

We all need and desire to be strong physically, emotionally, and spiritually. Our world has created a billion dollar drug industry that attempts to find a synthetic means by which we can feel strong in our bodies and our minds. It's merely a band-aid, but with everyone feeling weak and ready to hand over the cash for the cure, these companies flourish. Even with a list of horrible side effects, patients are not deterred from these prescriptions.

As Christians, we understand the only true strength that can never fail (and is only accompanied with positive side effects) is the strength that comes from God. Nehemiah 8:10 prescribes: The joy of the Lord is my strength. The Bible equates joy with strength, so if the joy of the Lord is our strength, then the absence of this joy is weakness. Is it any wonder the devil is in hot pursuit to steal our joy? He's not after your stuff; he's after your joy. He knows if he can whittle away at your attitude of joy, he can undermine your spiritual strength and even steal your witness to those around you.

It is not a very effective calling card for Christianity if we are moping around, constantly being swayed by the events of the world, complaining about our problems, unenthusiastically approaching our work, or yelling at the neighbor's dog simply because we are having a 'fat' day. The unsaved people around us will think, "That Jesus deal certainly isn't working out for them...they're no better off than I am. Maybe I should offer them some of my drugs?"

As Second Mile Christians, we must learn to walk in the power of God's joy every single day! No matter what the situation might be, our attitude is: "I am a child of the Most High God, the head and not the tail, above only and never beneath! I have been given all spiritual blessings, and the power to overcome every situation! I never give up or give in because I have the victory that overcomes the world, and Christ has given me all authority over the devil!" Now this kind of joy will draw some stares…and magnetize people to you. They will want what you have, and you will be able to offer the true prescription that will heal their souls.

SECOND MILE STRETCHES:
1. Awaken everyday with thanksgiving on your lips. Purpose to open your eyes and give praise to God for all He has done in your life and all He will do for you today.
2. Create habits that guard you against depression. Be aware of the strength of joy and sensitive to its departure in your heart. As soon as you begin to feel the heaviness of worry or anxiety, stop right there and begin to confess the blessings of God over your life.
3. Live bigger than yourself. Decide to be more concerned with your witness to others than the circumstances you might be facing.

NOTES:

SECTION THREE:
inward

We cannot give what we do not have. If we try, our attempts will only be shallow and superficial. Our pursuit of the Second Mile life must include an honest inspection of our hearts, willing and eager to join King David in his prayer, 'Create in me a clean heart, Oh God, And renew a steadfast spirit within me.' Only then will our dreams of significantly making a difference with our lives will be fulfilled.

CHAPTER FIVE

Courage

We call them "The Twelve." Around the world stand magnificent cathedrals erected in their names. Countless iconic statues, busts and larger-than-life sculptures of their likenesses, in mediums from the most rare marble to the cheapest lumber are sprinkled throughout churches, holy places and front lawns. Famous paintings by famous artists portray them strong and courageous, almost as Roman gods. Their names are 'household names,' and Christians and non-Christians alike from many nations christen their sons after these great men. There exist scores of historic books and novels written about their lives, and even the Veggie Tales franchise depicts these heroes in their cleverly animated movies.

"The Twelve." When we see the exploits of these notable men, we tend to idolize them and catalog them as super men, faster than speeding bullets and able to leap tall buildings in a single bound. To stack their lives up against ours today, we would be dwarfed by their images. And as the story of The Twelve unfolds in dramatic fashion, almost like a modern day movie, it is easy to imagine their lives and create a fairy tale adventure, a kind of make-believe fantasy.

I have always been intrigued by the assembly of men Jesus selected to be His apostles. Whenever I read their journey with Christ in the Gospels, I often step back in time and role-play, wondering which apostle I would have been if I had the opportunity to walk in their sandals. Would I be Peter "The Rock?" One of the "Sons of Thunder?" Or maybe, John "The Apostle of Love?"

However, we always have to remind ourselves that these amazing men did not start out that way. When we examine the information offered in the Gospels closely, we can clearly see how human The Twelve really were. These were just a group of simple men: some working-class, some businessmen, some very successful, some average, some middle-aged, and some very young. None, however, had prestige or power as the Roman officials or the Jewish Pharisees possessed; they were ordinary men who needed the grace of God to accomplish their extraordinary calling (just like you and me).

During their eighteen-month journey with Jesus, there were plenty of opportunities for them to expose their many shortcomings. Many times, they didn't seem to understand the point of some of the most valuable concepts Christ was trying to teach. One moment they would jockey for position, arguing over who was the greatest, and the next, they were found panicking with fear during a storm on the sea. They were arrogant, boasting foolishly of being able to drink of the same cup of suffering that Jesus would, only to end up betraying, abandoning and denying Him. They sometimes acted impulsively, they slept when they should have been awake, and they worried when they should have taken rest. The group included a traitor, a doubter, and a man who liked to cuss. And yet, the most imperative mission the planet would ever embrace—global evangelism and the continuation of the ministry of Jesus Christ—hinged entirely on these twelve men!

With that perspective, it's pretty amazing Jesus handpicked these men, in spite of their handicaps and inadequacies, to carry out the most vital assignment in world history. In fact, I find it to be quite encouraging to realize Jesus wasn't looking for perfectly manicured and educated all-stars whose talent and charisma would catch the eyes of the popular crowd; He was looking for surrendered people who could be used by God to capture the hearts of entire nations. The Bible tells us: *"The Lord doesn't make decisions the way (we) do. People judge by outward appearance, but the Lord looks at a person's thoughts and intentions of the heart." (I Samuel 16:7b, NLT).*

These men, ordinary as they might have been, were extraordinary in their hearts, for they emanated a quality that every Second Miler must possess…courage. Their willingness to relinquish everything they knew in order to follow and to promote Christ took extreme courage, and it set these men apart from the rest. They gave no regard for what their families or friends thought or for what the social norms were of their time. They never allowed fear to deflect them from their commitment to follow Jesus (save the crucifixion incident, which I doubt any of us would have responded differently). Their yearning for something more from God overshadowed any temptations to walk away from Him when they were filled with uncertainty or difficulty.

Courage was the quality Jesus saw in the ones He trusted to begin the evangelization of planet Earth, and courage is what He is looking for in us today. He does not see us for who we are at this moment, He sees us for who we can be. We only need to step out in valor and answer His call. No matter who you are, no matter where you come from, no matter what your past failures, all Jesus needs from you is a bold "Yes!" and He can transform you into more than you could ever ask or think. And before you start listing all of your inadequacies, all the reasons why God could not possibly make your life significant, keep reading…you are about to be very encouraged!

THE STRENGTH THAT YOU HAVE

By all accounts of his time, Gideon was definitely not the guy voted "Most Likely to Succeed" of his senior class. In fact, he probably was the guy who did not get nominated for any one of the "Most Likely" awards given away at prom…which was perhaps for the best anyway as he could not find himself a date for the event. He was the guy who flew under the radar, never standing out in any way; the one whose name nobody could ever remember or whose face they could only vaguely describe.

In the Book of Judges, chapter six, it says that Gideon, by his own admission, belonged to the family that was the weakest in the entire nation of Israel, and from amongst his siblings, he was the scrawniest and most pathetic. And this was at a time when Israel was at its lowest; they had forgotten The Lord their God, and as a result had been enslaved for generations by the merciless Midianites. Gideon was the least of the least and the lowest of the low. He didn't think very much of himself, and I'm sure there wasn't anyone around him trying to convince him otherwise...except maybe his mommy. I bet on top of it all he was a "momma's boy."

Then in verse twelve, the Angel of the Lord comes to Gideon who is threshing wheat inside a winepress, a job so dirty and dusty it is usually done in the open air. But he was hiding from the Midianites. The Angel boldly declares, *"The Lord is with you, mighty warrior!"* I'm sure Gideon must have looked over his shoulder to see whom this angel might have been referring to. It certainly could not be him...the guy who was almost indistinguishable in the cloud of dust from the indoor wheat threshing. Covered from head to toe in dust and debris, he begins to question the angel, doubting his words, and professing his apparent inadequacies. To this negative confession, the angel does not even respond; he neither agrees nor disagrees to Gideon's self-accusations. (I have always found this to be quite interesting. I wonder if upon seeing Gideon the angel felt compelled to check back with God to make sure he had the correct address and the right guy). Instead, God's messenger prophesies to Gideon that he will save his people by leading the Israelite army to defeat the Midianites, and simply tells him, *"Go in the strength that you have...The Lord will be with you."*

Go in the strength that you have. That's an awesome statement, and can change your life if you let it penetrate your heart. If these words would have been placed in one of the Psalms, I'm certain the sentence would be followed by a 'Selah,' which means, 'pause and calmly meditate on this.' The angel did not quantify how much strength Gideon needed, he merely told him to go with whatever strength he did have…no matter how miniscule it might have been. God saw something within Gideon's heart that he did not know was there, or at least that he had forgotten was there. God saw courage, and just like The Twelve, He gave him an opportunity to step out in faith to do something great for his generation.

Gideon answers the call with a heroic "Yes!" and miraculous events begin to occur. The next two chapters reveal a completely different Gideon; he begins to see himself as God sees him, and with only three hundred men, he totally annihilates the Midianite army. God is faithful to go before the Israelite army as not one of Gideon's men are killed, while over one hundred twenty thousand of the enemy's men fall. The destruction is so complete, and the victory so unbelievable, that the nation of Israel cannot deny the mighty Hand of God. They all renew their relationship with God, and worship Him as the One and Only. One man—one weak, unpopular, forgotten man—turned the heart of an entire nation back to God simply by having the courage to say "yes" to God.

Throughout the Bible, we see scores of heroes and heroines who were completely inadequate in their own strength, unlikely to be the 'chosen ones' by God, and yet because of their courage to trust in God to fulfill His promises within them, they are now recorded in the History of Eternity. In fact, as you study their stories, you will find that almost all of them felt insufficient at one time or another, and many of them even made some serious mistakes along the way…but they did not give up and today they are 'household names.' I wonder how many people since the creation of Adam and Eve have been called by God to achieve something great for His kingdom, but because their shortcomings were bigger in their eyes than the power of God, they answered "no" to the invitation? We will never know because they are not mentioned in The Book.

A COURAGEOUS 'YES'

Every one of us has an opportunity to be a part of changing the hearts of our neighborhood, our cities, our nations, our generations, our world. The only thing that can stop us from accomplishing the true destiny God has planned for us is our answer to His call. And as we can see in Gideon and the twelve apostles, we don't need to wait until we 'have it all together,' and until we've fixed all of our apparent weaknesses. Jesus doesn't choose the perfect; He chooses the Second Milers who dare to be courageous and authentic. Scripture tells us: *"Few of you were wise in the world's eyes, or powerful, or wealthy when God called you. Instead, God deliberately chose things the world considers foolish in order to shame those who think they are wise. And He chose those who are powerless to shame those who are powerful. God chose things despised by the world, things counted as nothing at all, and used them to bring to nothing what the world considers important, so that no one can ever boast in the presence of God."* (I Corinthians 1: 26-29, NLT).

I can certainly vouch for this! I'm just a guy who grew up in a tiny town in Southeast Missouri (seriously, I think our town census included large pets just to be able to have more than a 3 digit total on our welcome sign). I had no pedigree, no connections, no wealth. But I did have a heart to serve God, and when I eventually entered into ministry over fourteen years ago, I started with twelve guys on a basketball team; that was my first church! I didn't wait for a title, a job description, or a salary; I simply started with what was available to me. With zero training, I didn't know what I was doing, and I made plenty of mistakes as I attempted to pastor and mentor these young men. There were many risks involved, personally and materialistically, but I have never regretted saying "yes" to God. I went in the strength that I had, and throughout the years, God has blessed me with more influence and more people as I have allowed Him to enlarge my heart with His vision. I may never become a 'household name' on this earth, but I am determined to live a Second Mile life that will impact heaven, one that will help and serve people and make eternal ripples in God's Kingdom.

The Second Mile takes courage, and even if, like Gideon, you have forgotten the meat of who you really are, as you step out in faith and turn your attention to how great God is, you will find yourself being transformed. Every one of us has doubts. As soon as we begin to tap into the kingdom potential inside us, our minds are assaulted with all the reasons why God could never use us like He did our Bible heroes. We have a complete file system of excuses, and we say things like, "Well, I just can't." But God declares, *"You can do all things through Christ who gives strength to you" (Phil. 4:13)* We make a list of the things we don't have when God's Word says, *"He has given us everything that pertains to life and godliness" (2 Peter 1:3)*. We think it is totally impossible, while God reminds us, *"With men it's impossible, but with God all things are possible" (Mark 9:23)*. We tell Him of everything we used to be and all our past failures, but He says, *"Old things are passed away and all things are new" (2 Corinthians 5:17)*

> # God will give you the strength that you need.

It's time to believe in God's Word more than you believe in your doubts and in your limitations. Let's quit telling God everything we are not and open up our eyes to everything He is! Every great man or woman of God had issues...many could have been perfect candidates for *The Jerry Springer Show,* but God used them in spite of their 'issues.' All He asks is that we have the courage to go in the strength that we have.

He will make up the rest. I cannot tell you how many times I have found myself in a size 10 situation, and I was only a size 4 $^1/_2$. But never has there been a time when I have trusted in God to make up the difference and He let me down...Never! He will do the same for you.

Let's get a vision for what our life, our careers, our relationships, our futures would look like if we simply went in with the strength that we had. Excuses will keep your rear-end super glued to your seat and your name out of the History of Eternity. Having the courage to step out, trust God and lean into your true destiny will give you a front row roller coaster seat to the supernatural outpouring of God! It only takes one step to get into that first car on the Second Mile ride, to just say "yes" to God...and then strap in, hang on, and get ready for the thrill of a lifetime!

CHAPTER SIX

Forgiveness

Forgiveness is one of the most powerful forces in the world today. For Christians, it is the nucleus of our faith and the turning point of our eternal destiny. When you receive the forgiveness of God for your sins, it changes everything about you. It frees you from the guilt and shame of your past, washes you from the incriminating stains of your present, and launches you into God's glorious plans for your future. The Bible consistently describes the character and nature of God as being merciful and compassionate, pointing to His desire to offer forgiveness. David recognized this in the psalms by saying, *"O Lord, you are so good, so ready to forgive, so full of unfailing love for all who ask your aid."*

All of us have great need of God's gift of forgiveness. Amazingly, He offers us this gift not based on our own merits, but on what Jesus accomplished for us on the Cross. By laying down His life, the perfect Lamb of God took upon Himself the sins of the world and received the full punishment our sinfulness required. It was such a simple plan, but it demanded an unaffordable price, and Jesus paid it; all we must do is receive it. As a result, our sin-debt has been cancelled and its penalty has been removed. Life change now turns out to be possible for us and, even more incredibly, heaven becomes available to us.

One would think that after receiving so great a gift motivated by such amazing love, it would be no problem to reciprocate this generosity of forgiveness to everyone we meet. One would think, but that sure is not the case, is it? It is easy for me to embrace forgiveness when I am the one who stands in need of it. But when I am faced with a situation when I must offer it to someone else who has mistreated me, forgiveness can become much more of a challenge. And once again, we encounter the difference between the First Mile life and the Second Mile life. Faith for the First Mile will enable us to confess our own sins and receive God's forgiveness of them. Faith for the Second Mile will insist that we forgive those who have hurt and offended us.

WHAT FORGIVENESS IS NOT

As we unpack this idea of what forgiveness is, it may help us to first determine what forgiveness is not. Forgiveness is not an attempt to "gloss over" or minimize your own pain. When someone else hurts you, forgiveness does not mean you ignore your injury and act like the offense came at no cost to you. You do not have to talk yourself out of what happened or pretend that your pain does not exist. In order to fully forgive and begin the process of healing, you must first be honest with the extent of your hurt.

Forgiveness is not approving the actions of your perpetrator. Sometimes, we may be reluctant to forgive our offenders because in doing so, we may feel like we are endorsing their behavior. Do not confuse forgiveness with approval. Forgiveness does not turn a blind eye and say, "It's no big deal. What you did to me was okay." Forgiveness fully recognizes the wrongness of someone else's actions.

On the heels of that statement, let me insert that forgiveness is not an invitation to be someone else's doormat. A forgiving spirit does not mean you have to open yourself up to circumstances of which you might be taken advantage. You can cancel the debt of someone who has mistreated you without having to put yourself in the position of being a victim again. Forgiving the people who hurt us does not require us to turn around and be their best friends.

While it may be true that time can heal many wounds, time alone is not enough to restore someone's life. Forgiveness is not something passive—just waiting the problem out in hopes of one day getting over it. Second Mile forgiveness is a very active, intentional choice that will enable us to live in freedom and wholeness.

In addition, and perhaps most importantly, forgiveness does not hinge on the cooperation of your offender. We tend to withhold forgiveness, at times, because we expect some kind of admission of guilt on their part. We think, "I did nothing wrong. He is the one who started all of this. It's his responsibility to make things right. He owes me an apology first." If this is our attitude, we can spend our entire life waiting in bitterness and resentfulness at his or her unwillingness to acknowledge their sin and repent. We can wait for the apology that may never come.

I have counseled with people who withhold forgiveness in an effort to punish their perpetrators, and I have witnessed firsthand the destruction this creates. Instead of penalizing their offenders, they are really only hurting themselves. When you barricade your heart to keep others out, you also set up boundaries that lock you in. Ironically, the walls of your protection turn into the walls of your own prison. New friendships become difficult to form because of old hurts that have never been healed. All the while, their perpetrators unknowingly move forward in their lives.

In my experience, I have learned that when I am offended or have gotten my feelings hurt by someone else, most of the time that other person never even intended to do it. Remember Jesus' prayer from the Cross: *"Father, forgive them for they do not even know what they are doing."* My offender may have no idea what he has done or how his actions made me feel, and here I am, holding him accountable to a transgression of which he is not even aware. Even in situations where the wrongdoing is severe and abusive, many times the perpetrator is so entangled with his own sin, suffocating in his own pain, he is blind to anything else. In these tragic cases, forgiveness is still necessary for you to be freed from the darkness of those memories, but this kind of forgiveness comes with great prayer and wise counsel.

We can easily put unrealistic expectations on people, requiring them to fix a breakdown they do not even know exists. They are not aware of the problem, we refuse to address the problem, and the relationship begins to wilt because of neglect. The Bible has a remedy for this kind of stalemate. Jesus commands us, in Matthew, chapter eighteen, to go privately to the one who has offended us and point out the problem for the purpose of reconciliation. It is amazing what we can work out when our communication is clear and direct.

Notice that Jesus does not give us permission to discuss the issue with everyone else until we go to our offender first. If our hearts are pure, and we need to have a conversation with someone about the best way to approach the situation, that's one thing. It is another thing entirely, if out of a heart of revenge or self-pity, we go running to the phone to inform our best friends of how we have been wronged. This might feel easier than confronting our offender with the spirit of Christ, but the more we talk about the problem to others, the bigger it grows! Not only that, but we allow those around us to take up our offense. This kind of action is completely out of bounds from the parameters in which God has set. We complicate an already sticky situation when we "three-way" our offender by bringing in a third party without having talked to him first.

Second Mile forgiveness requires more effort and energy to approach the one who wronged us than it does to sit back and mentally or verbally pick him/her apart. The value you place on your friendships will be seen in your willingness to biblically nurture them. Spirit-led confrontation and communication are vital parts of any healthy bond. Nobody likes confrontation, including me (I get red splotches on my neck and battle nausea when I have to do it), and all of us have to fight against the temptation to avoid the person and situation altogether. But if we give in to the 'easy road,' we will lose a potentially valuable, life-giving friendship because we were not willing to do what the Bible says.

WHAT FORGIVENESS IS

As you can see, forgiveness involves sorting through many formidable thoughts and feelings—thoughts and feelings we believe to be completely justified. Regardless of how legitimate they may be, we cannot exalt our own opinions above the requirements God has set forth in His Word. Forgiveness is something supernatural; willpower, determination, or human effort alone cannot accomplish it, although all three of these are needed in order to courageously operate in it.

Forgiveness flows from the Spirit of Christ, and only those who have been forgiven by Him truly know how to forgive. If you have not tapped into God's forgiveness, you will never know how to cancel someone else's debt. Ephesians 4:31-32 says, *"Get rid of all bitterness, rage, anger, harsh words, and slander, as well as all types of malicious behavior. Instead, be kind to each other, tenderhearted, forgiving one another, just as God through Christ has forgiven you."* (NLT)

The Cross is the only way we can receive true forgiveness and offer it to those who have wronged us. God will never require us to cancel the debt of another that is greater than the collective one we owed to Him. Sometimes, in our 'born-again,' saved lives, we tend to minimize the state of sin we were in before we accepted Jesus' sacrifice, while magnifying the sin someone did to us. On the contrary, all of the acts committed against us must be viewed through the lens of our own personal need for His mercy and forgiveness.

When we understand the extent of our own sinfulness, we have a better perspective on how to deal with the sins of others. Jesus instructed His disciples to pray, "Forgive us our sins, *just* as we have forgiven those who have sinned against us." We must forgive others to the exact same degree we want God to forgive us. If I want God to take my sins and throw them into His Sea of forgetfulness, I cannot afford to hold onto the faults of those who mistreat me.

THE POWER OF FORGIVENESS

The person with a forgiving spirit not only pardons his debtor but also frees himself. George Washington Carver once said, "I will never let another man ruin my life by making me hate him." Painful memories have a way of tying us to the past and keeping us locked up in resentment. By forgiving others, we sever the cords that keep us stuck in a painful moment of the past and we free ourselves to move forward in our relationships. Refusing to keep track of offenses will always keep us in the race and give us longevity to go the Second Mile.

Unconditional forgiveness says to its offenders, "I release you, and I don't expect anything from you. You owe me nothing...not even an apology." Regardless of our innocence or how undeserving our offender may be, by choosing to forgive, we stop the process of destruction and start the process of healing. We become empowered as we cast off our role as a victim and bravely take on the responsibility of healing our pain. Instead of being at the mercy of someone else, we are now in the driver's seat, and we can victoriously move forward with the Holy Spirit, our Comforter, to complete wholeness and freedom within our souls.

> **If I want God to take my sins and throw them into His Sea of forgetfulness, I cannot afford to hold onto the faults of those who mistreat me.**

When my oldest daughter was in pre-school, I looked forward to dropping her off in the morning and picking her up in the afternoon because it meant uninterrupted time together. We prayed together, giggled together, listened to our favorite songs, and shared the events of the day. On one afternoon, she jumped into my car with a pair of huge, elephant-like ears around her head. Bubbling with excitement she said, "Hey, Daddy, do you like my ears? These are my new listening ears!" She was proud of her artwork, and I was impressed with her creativity.

As we began to discuss her day, I noticed through my rearview mirror that her countenance began to change. With a frown on her face she reported, "Daddy, someone was mean to me at recess today. A little girl told me that she hated my guts and wanted to cut my head off!"

I was shocked! A little four-year-old girl talking like that must be watching too much television at home...either that, or she had a few older brothers.

"Did you tell your teacher?" I asked.

"Yes sir," she responded.

"Did the little girl get in trouble?" I continued.

"Yes sir," she repeated.

"Well, what happened next?" I pressed. At this point, Alexa pulled her listening ears over her face so she would not have to look at me. "Daddy, I don't want to tell you...I want to tell Mommy!"

I reassured her that it was okay and that her answer was safe with me. After much negotiating and coaxing, Alexa finally confessed, "Well...me and some of my friends...we picked up a bunch of rocks... and started throwing them at her!" The truth was out and the deluge of tears was in full force.

Now, I wish I could say I reacted to her news of the day in the perfect expression of our merciful and forgiving Lord. Instead, my first thoughts and feelings were of a very human, protective daddy. *How dare that girl say such cruel words to my Alexa! I want some retribution* here. *I wonder if any of those rocks actually hit their target?! That was when I caught myself. Get a hold of yourself, man!* I knew that no matter what that girl said to Alexa, it was unacceptable for her to not only respond in such a way, but also, to rally her friends to join her. At that moment, I was thinking justice for one, not justice for all.

After calming myself down, I turned to her and gently reminded her, "Baby, we never throw rocks at others, even if they say mean things to us. We're going to do two things: First of all, we are going to pray and ask Jesus to forgive us for throwing rocks. Second, when you go back to school tomorrow, you are going to find this little girl and tell her you are sorry for what you did."

As Alexa and I talked to Jesus, asking Him to forgive her for what she had done, something very unexpected stirred within my heart. The Holy Spirit began to talk to me about my own life, and how my daughter was not the only expert rock-thrower in the family. In my past, I also had tossed many emotional rocks of revenge, determined to punish the people who had mistreated me. I could see that young man picking up stones of anger, resentment, bitterness, and rage then mercilessly hurling them at my perpetrators, vowing to never be hurt again. In an instant, I understood how exhausting and useless it is to retaliate in anger. No matter how hard you try, you never can collect (or throw) enough rocks to settle the score anyway.

Have you ever seen one of those suspense movies where the plot has so many twists and turns that you don't have a full understanding of the whole thing until the very last moment? In hindsight, as you replay the events and the conversations of the characters in your mind, everything suddenly becomes crystal clear. This moment with the Holy Spirit was very much like that. He showed me how burdened down I had been in my past, shouldering the load of heavy, 'unforgiveness' boulders, and how over the past decade, He had been working in my heart bit by bit to chisel away at the monument I had created.

As a teenager, I was fully on fire for the things of God and I had committed myself spiritually, emotionally, and socially to the involvement of my church. I had a wonderful youth pastor who took me under his wing and was (and still is) the most significant mentor in my life. Then in a matter of a few months, there was a complete disintegration of the large church in which I was involved; I watched in dismay as my youth pastor was unjustly released, and as the higher leadership was exposed of dishonesty, greed, and other grave sin. The entire ministry was turned upside down, and there were many, many Christians left wounded and without a shepherd from the wake of this destruction.

I was shell-shocked. A person can be expected to be hurt from the world, but Church is supposed to be a place of safety, a refuge to come to in order to freely be vulnerable and to grow spirit, soul and body. It's one thing to feel betrayed by someone who has never claimed to be a person of integrity, but it's entirely another thing to be deceived by a leader who preaches the Word of God and urges all of his flock to live a life of holiness. At such an impressionable age, these wounds ran deep into my soul.

Then not long after, my parents announced they were getting divorced. This was the knockout blow from the devil's "One-Two Punch." Once again, I faced betrayal and abandonment from the people who were supposed to be guardians in my life, and I felt as though everything I thought to be my secure foundation was really just a field of sinking sand. I didn't know who I could trust anymore, who I could look up to, and as a result, I made the decision to go it alone with God. My beliefs about Him had not changed; He was the only one I knew I could count on. So there I went along my path, laden with huge stones of unforgiveness, away from church and my dreams of impacting the world through ministry. Luckily, my plans of being the lone wolf were not God's plans...

A few years later, I came into contact with my former youth pastor who now was pastoring his own church, and he asked me to come and join him in the vision. He invited both Rachel and me to help build the youth ministry of what is now Healing Place Church, and although we were just married, we knew this was the call of God. I am ever thankful for this opportunity because it ultimately saved my life, 'soulishly' speaking. We became so entrenched in the work of building a great youth ministry, that my hands, which were now thoroughly occupied with the work of the church, were no longer tightly clasped around those terrible rocks. The Holy Spirit was now free to begin a work deep in my heart.

Over the next years, as I grew in spiritual maturity and continued to commit myself to God's plan for my life, He began to show me bit by bit how to receive healing for the deep-seated bitterness and distrust I had allowed to take root in my heart. He taught me how to truly forgive, how to fully trust people again (especially those in leadership over me), and how to surrender any secret hopes for retribution I might have been holding on to. God is so gracious and patient; He doesn't try to overhaul our emotional issues all at once because He knows we could not handle that. He's such a gentleman, and He walks us through our valleys of pain to the broad, open space of freedom at our own pace.

Life becomes heavy when our pockets are full of rocks.

That day with Alexa, as we prayed for forgiveness and I had a true encounter with the Holy Spirit, was a significant day for me. Like the end of that movie I described earlier, this was the 'Aha!' moment for me. He reminded me of my past self, so bent over from the load of unforgiveness, and He revealed to me how He had been working on my heart to bring me to a place of total freedom. He showed me how every time I was faithful to respond to His promptings over the years to build relationships, to operate in grace and trust for people, to faithfully serve God's people, He had all the while been chiseling away at those stones. With this hindsight, I was able to recall how oppressed I had been years ago and to compare that past self to my present self, and it was at that moment when I realized that my pockets were completely empty! This realization of the victory and freedom that had been accruing in my soul was exhilarating. I knew at that moment, that I would never again allow myself to harbor the weight of unforgiveness towards any person for any reason. The cost of that burden was simply not worth it.

Life becomes heavy when our pockets are full of rocks. Jesus never intended for us to be weighed down with the burden of avenging our own pain. That is why He told us that vengeance belongs to Him—He will repay. If you find yourself, as you read this book, recognizing that you are under the heavy weight of unforgiveness, I urge you to make the choice to, as the famous phrase says: Let Go, and Let God! If I can do it, you certainly can, and with the help of the Holy Spirit, you will be able to find a weightless freedom in your life you never thought possible. No matter how large the offense was, God can and will walk you through the process, step by step, never allowing you to become overwhelmed. He can be trusted.

Remember, unconditional forgiveness says to its offenders, "I release you, and I don't expect anything from you. You owe me nothing... not even an apology." Many times this type of forgiveness is only possible through the strength of the Holy Spirit, but it is possible. It is only by refusing to keep track of offenses within your heart that you will be able to stay in the race and possess the longevity to go the Second Mile. It's time to let go of the rocks!

CHAPTER SEVEN

Perseverance

In Chapter 37 of the Book of Genesis, we meet a famous Bible hero, and an authentic Second Miler, Joseph. Talk about a 'household name'... this man has had many movies made about him, including a smash-hit Andrew Lloyd Webber musical, *Joseph and the Amazing Techni-Colored Dream Coat*. In addition, he is one of the most popular Biblical characters used in sermons. He is the ultimate example of the 'Cinderella' story, the bad news/good news testimony, the epitome of the Comeback Kid. He was one of the twelve sons of Jacob (imagine the craziness around that dinner table with all those boys...you'd risk losing a hand trying to grab the last chicken wing), and although he was the most beloved son of his father, he was the least liked amongst his jealous brothers. True, Joseph brought some of this fraternal hatred upon himself as he tattled bad reports of his siblings to his father, strutted around in a not-so-modest coat of many colors especially made for him by his father, and blurted prophetic dreams to them about how one day he would rule over them. But even in his youth and immaturity, he certainly did not deserve the awful fate of the next twenty-two years set in motion by his revengeful older brothers.

Plotting Joseph's demise, the brothers decided to kill him and tell their father that a wild beast had fatally attacked him. However, their plan quickly changed upon seeing a profit could be made, and they chose instead to sell him as a slave to a clan of Ishmaelite traders passing by on their journey to Egypt. Thus began over two decades of a life for Joseph far from the protected, favored life he had been experiencing. First, he is sold as a slave to Potiphar, an officer of Pharaoh, and serves his way to the top of the staff only to be falsely accused of sexual assault by Potiphar's wife. Then he is thrown into prison where he remains abandoned for many years as he fills his time serving the prison guard. There he encounters two of Pharaoh's key employees, a baker and a butler, who are being punished by the king. Each of them have been having strange, re-occurring dreams and they ask if Joseph has any insight into the dreams' meanings. He accurately interprets their dreams, and the butler is so overjoyed with the outcome, he promises to mention Joseph to Pharaoh and to help him get released from prison. However, the butler promptly forgets about Joseph. It is not until three years later when a string of dreams are haunting Pharaoh that the butler remembers Joseph's interpreting skills. Joseph is summoned to Pharaoh, illuminates the meaning of the dreams, and 'suddenly' becomes Pharaoh's right-hand-man, the second in command over the entire nation of Egypt. (I realize this is an incredibly condensed, Reader's Digest version of the story, but you can fill in the details by reading the account in Genesis, starting with Chapter 37.)

Even though the end of the story is exciting, for many years prior, Joseph was a victim of terrible circumstances. He was betrayed, abandoned, lied about, forgotten, used and abused. His story from prison to palace, which takes us about twenty-two minutes to read, was actually an agonizing twenty-two years! He could have hosted quite a pity party for himself and many would have come to empathize with his pain. He could have lost himself in a life of alcoholism, anger and bitterness. He could have thrown up a violent fist at God and blamed Him for all his misfortunes. But had he acted like this and given up on his dreams, as many of us probably would have been tempted to do, he never would have seen them come to pass. He only would have gotten a few verses of mention in the Old Testament (instead of the dozen chapters dedicated to his life), and the whole of Egypt, consisting of millions and millions of people, would have experienced utter ruin.

No, Joseph was a Second Miler. Within his character, we find a key ingredient every person desiring to experience the Second Mile life must possess...perseverance. Despite the many problems, difficulties, pains and abuses, Joseph steadily persisted through them all. He demanded his heart to remain stable, solidly trusting in God, even when everything around him was falling apart. He never gave in to the temptation to wallow in self-pity, to complain, and to give up. As a result, the Bible tells us repeatedly that the favor of God was upon Joseph's life, and everywhere he was placed, he rose to the highest potential of that post. In a world where unfair things happen, we all need to emulate this quality of perseverance if we are to acquire and to enjoy a Second Mile life.

> **Our relationship with Jesus does not guarantee us a trouble-free life.**

ABOVE THE STORM

Many times when we become a Christian, whether it be as a small child or in our adult years, we are so happy to be in the family of God and to be assured of our place in heaven, we fail to remember we are currently abiding on Earth. Excited to be understanding the Word of God, and beginning to see His blessings work in our lives, we can become lulled into thinking because we have Jesus in our hearts we are completely free of the fallen state of the world in which we live. Unfortunately, our relationship with Jesus does not guarantee us a trouble-free life as we ride off into the sunset of eternal bliss and happiness. It does, however, promise that we will never have to go through another painful day all by ourselves. He vows to never leave us nor forsake us and although we might face trials and tribulations, He will lead us through to victory. In John 16:33, Jesus tells us, *"In this world you will have trouble. But take heart! I have overcome the world."(NIV)*

A lack of understanding in this area is what keeps many Christians living in the First Mile. Some of us have been completely shocked when a storm of life has actually dared to tread upon our pristine lawns, and as a result, have allowed ourselves to be shaken to the very core of our faith. But, we cannot fully explore the idea of following Christ's command to go the Second Mile without a conversation about the fact that part of the deal will include wading through some troubled waters. Hurt and suffering are part of the cursed world in which we live, and if you have a pulse, you will eventually experience pain, whether it is physical, mental, emotional, or spiritual. Regardless of how tropical the forecast may be, there is not a place on earth you can go to avoid the storm clouds of pain.

> **There is not a place on earth you can go to avoid the storm clouds of pain.**

Perseverance is crucial to weathering these storms. In fact, many times it is through our perseverance, our out-lasting the negative circumstances, where the very metal of our character is formed. Joseph is a perfect example of this; with each challenge that came his way, he set his focus on the promises of God and never allowed himself to become consumed by his trials. He allowed each experience to mold his character, to strengthen his will, and to affirm his faith rather than weaken his resolve to be all that he could be. Because of his perseverance, his heart was enlarged to a place where he was able to handle the responsibility and the stress of leading the most powerful country of the then known world. Joseph truly had a revelation of the yet unwritten scripture in the first chapter of James, *"Consider it pure joy, my brothers, whenever you face trials of many kinds, because you know that the testing of your faith develops perseverance. Perseverance must finish its work so that you may be mature and complete, not lacking anything."(James 1:2-4, NIV)*

Every one of us will face unfortunate, challenging, and sometimes incredibly unfair circumstances. I wish I could guarantee you a different truth, but that truth would really be a lie. The reality is some of us have been the victim of abuse as a child or adolescent and have carried guilt and shame into our adulthood. Some of us are trying to heal from the sting of a broken relationship; after years of commitment and trust, what we thought would last a lifetime is now falling down all around us. Some have been made fun of as a kid, or always picked last in sports, or felt like we grew up in the vapor trail of a successful older sibling. Some have just learned that a close friend is struggling with homosexuality, and we are at a total loss on how to respond. Some are under the heavy burden of bankruptcy, the loss of a job, or foreclosure of a home. Some have watched a beloved friend or family member fight a lengthy battle with cancer, and after many sleepless nights and prayers offered to heaven, we saw them slip away into eternity.

In these times of crisis, it is vital that we make the choice to press into our relationship with Christ rather than to allow the calamity to create doubts that drive us away from our very Source of Help. So often in our weakness, we tune our ears to formidable questions like: Is God the source of my pain? Is He doing this to teach me a lesson? Why do bad things happen to good people? If He is all-powerful, why didn't He prevent this from happening? Questions like these defeat our faith and weaken our ability to draw upon the power of God to overcome. Questions like these that require infinite wisdom to answer have no finite answers for us to grab hold of and only serve to unravel our trust in

Christ, and hinder our capacity to persevere. Questions like these keep us in the First Mile.

The Second Mile Christian cannot base his or her relationship with Jesus upon answers to questions or doubts. We must base our faith upon the truth of His Word, His Word that though heaven and earth will pass away, it will never pass away (Luke 21:33). Our trust is upon the Jesus who is the same yesterday, today and forever, and Who promises us that He will never leave nor forsake us (Hebrews 13:5,8). We do not pursue answers to doubtful questions; instead, we are in constant pursuit of the truth that can only be revealed through God's Word. And in this authentic search for truth, we will always find ourselves consumed with Jesus Who is the Way, the Truth, and the Life (John 14:6). Not a bad place to be in a time of trial.

GOD CAN TURN IT INTO GOOD

Growing up, I had the All-American experience—parents who loved me, grandparents who hugged me, and sisters who bugged me. My earliest memories revolve around church and church activities—Sunday school, Vacation Bible School, summer camps. We attended church at least three times a week where my dad served as choir director and minister of music. My life was nice, neat and wrinkle-free, and I thought Beaver Cleaver had nothing on me. All the pieces of the puzzle fit together perfectly until I learned that after twenty-two years of marriage, my parents were getting a divorce.

Suddenly, the safe Christian bubble I lived in for eighteen years had now become compromised. This was not supposed to happen to God-fearing, church-going people with family values. What about everything I had been taught concerning commitment, trust, and faithfulness? Divorce was something bad that happened to other kids' parents, not mine. I felt trapped in a nightmare I just could not wake up from. Life no longer made sense to me...and neither did God.

Nobody asked me how I felt about divorce. The decision had already been made, and I was forced to live with it. I had been hit by the shrapnel of circumstances beyond my control and was trying to find a way to stop the bleeding. My mind was confronted with questions in which I had no answers, and my emotions took me on a serious rollercoaster ride. I felt completely helpless and out of control. I went from shock and disbelief to anger and denial, eventually coming to the dead end of depression. Someone had stolen the happy ending from my life and I desperately wanted it back. Every crutch that I used to prop myself up had been yanked out from under me. I was crushed, skeptical, and reluctant to believe in anything.

> **Suddenly, the safe Christian bubble I lived in for eighteen years had now become compromised.**

I found myself at a crossroads. One path was calling me to give in to the temptation to just 'cut off' all the people who had hurt me and start fresh. Find a new path, new friends, a new faith, and most of all a new vow to trust the only person I knew would never hurt me: myself. The other path was not so appealing. This one urged me to walk through this storm, to persevere through the pain, and to learn to love and forgive everyone whom I felt had let me down, and above all press in to Jesus. The first path definitely seemed the easier of the two.

Studies show that in times of pressure and crisis, our human tendency is to revert to habit. Life throws us an unfamiliar curve, and we retreat to the familiar for comfort and security. In order to cope, we instinctively do the things we have routinely practiced time and time again. Luckily, I had established a network of Biblical habits within my heart because these habits would not allow me to choose that first path. With my future uncertain and my family falling apart, I ran for safety to the only shelter I knew could protect me, God Himself. In His presence, I began to embrace the severity of my pain and the significance of His healing power.

With Joseph as my model, I was determined to keep my heart anchored in my faith in God's Word as best I could, and because I responded to the crisis in this way, God was able to use it to bring maturity to my soul. As I look with hindsight, I see how that furnace of affliction taught me some valuable lessons about who God is when I am suffering. These are revelations I never would have been able to grasp had I decided to settle for an escape route instead of walking through the shadowy valley. I learned that God did not cause my parents' marriage to disintegrate into divorce. He is never the source of our pain—how can He be when the essence of Who He is is pure Life and Light? He does, however, have the ability to use the painful things we go through for our good and His glory…if we allow Him to do so. Romans, chapter eight tells us, *"And we know that all things work together for the good of those who love God and are called according to His purpose." (Romans 8:28, NKJV)* Notice how the Bible does not say that all things are good, but that He has the ability to work all things (including the bad) for our good. I also learned that no matter what is happening around me, I must always keep a heart of gratitude and trust toward my Father in heaven, praising Him for His faithfulness regardless of how I feel.

Making a decision to persevere and to declare the goodness of God in the middle of your anything-but-good circumstances is not the easiest thing to do, but it is what is required of the Second Miler. And trust me, if I can do it, you certainly can too. All throughout Scripture, men and women of faith have been compelled to do just that, and as we learned in the previous chapter on worship, it is in this attitude our power to overcome is revealed. Joseph was betrayed by his own brothers, framed and falsely accused, and left to rot in a foreign prison. Yet, when he came face-to-face with the perpetrators of his pain he declared, "As far as I am concerned, God turned into good what you meant for evil. He brought me to the high position I have today so I could save the lives of many people." Wow! Joseph inspires me to reach for God's perspective, for God's way of doing things.

What is it that enables us to resist blaming God and to avoid hating the people who hurt us? It is nothing less than the supernatural power of the Holy Spirit. Only through His strength working within our hearts can we believe the promises that God is good and ever faithful, even when our circumstances attempt to convince us otherwise. The Holy Spirit comforts us and reminds us that God passionately loves us, ordering our every step for us so that we will never slide down a slippery slope of destruction. He gives us the courage to persevere through the tempests of life, to patiently wait for the sun to shine again, and to use the wisdom we gained in the midst of our storm to in turn lead other people through their own devastation to a place of triumph.

You are never alone. Regardless of what you have gone through, what challenges you might be enduring at this very moment, no matter how hopeless the situation might seem or how helpless you are feeling, one thing is certain: you can put your faith in the God who has ordered your every step and already has provided for you a way of escape. In addition, of all the things there are to love about God, perhaps His redemptive ability stands out most. I am amazed how God will not only offer us everything we need to be able to overcome, but also, He will never waste a single painful experience we go through. With Him, there is no such thing as meaningless suffering.

The psalmist David wrote, *"You keep track of all my sorrows. You have collected all my tears in your bottle. You have recorded each one in your book...This I know: God is on my side."* (Psalm 56:8-9, NLT) I find it interesting that God promises to forget our sins when we repent (Isaiah 43:25), but here tells us He keeps a ledger of all our pain. Why does

God forget our sins but always remember our sorrows? I believe God *records* it so He can *redeem* it! Just like Joseph testified to his brothers, when evil comes our way, if we will surrender ourselves to God, He will take that circumstance and turn it around for good. Only God can take the worst thing that has happened to us and transform it into the best thing for us. He can make it benefit our own spiritual maturity and strengthen us to use that wisdom to help someone else get out of the crisis they are facing.

Isn't that just like God, to use the pain of our past to produce hope for someone else's future? Our most effective ministry so often comes out of our deepest pain, because only when we truly know what it is like to hurt, can we offer healing to someone else in sorrow and grief. The Second Miler understands this and when tribulation enters the scene, he knows he must persevere, not just for himself, but also for the sake of all the other people he will be able to minister to once he has come to a place of victory. The Second Miler does not shirk away from challenges because he knows they will not weaken him; he trusts God will utilize every detail to deepen his faith and strengthen his resolve to be a world changer. The Second Miler eats trials and tribulations for breakfast!

EVERY LAP COUNTS

SECTION THREE // LAP ONE

Focus and Passion

"No, dear brothers and sisters, I am still not all I should be, but I am focusing all my energies on this one thing: Forgetting the past and looking forward to what lies ahead, I strain to reach the end of the race and receive the prize for which God, through Jesus Christ, is calling us up to heaven." Philippians 3:13-14 NLT

Notice Paul said this one thing I do, not the forty things I dabble in. He was focused on keeping his eyes upon Jesus because he knew it was the only way he would have the wisdom and discernment to fulfill the mission of his ministry. I believe Paul was able to stay so focused because he never allowed his passion for the work of Christ to become diluted or double minded.

Identifying what our passions are is important if we are going to live a life of focus and purpose. Have you noticed how easy it is to get distracted in today's culture? Every single day, we are faced with decisions on how we will spend our time and energy, and with those choices are trade-offs. We must handle the challenge of balancing marriage, children, checkbooks, careers, friendships, leisure time, and many other responsibilities. Passion is like a compass that will help you stay on mission.

Jesus stayed on mission because He was passionate about doing the will of the Father. In the Gospel of John alone, Jesus is recorded 47 different times saying, "I must be about my Father's business." His life was one holy interruption after another, and the temptation to be pulled in multiple directions was always there. Yet, it was focused passion that navigated Him through the crazy maze of society and the impure motives of man.

When we know what our God-given passions are, we can be confident we are walking through doors that God Himself is opening and know that He will give us the grace to do it. We will also be able to recognize the things that consume our time and suck us into the vortex of busyness. Do you have a hard time telling people "No"? If you feel like you have to say "Yes" to everyone and everything, you will end up a very frantic and ineffective person. Guilt and approval are terrible masters! When you strive to keep everyone happy, you end up making no one happy, including yourself! Passion is the compass that allows you to stay focused, to say "yes" with conviction and "no" without guilt.

SECOND MILE STRETCHES:
Take some time to evaluate your schedule:
1. Are your daily activities moving you forward in your God-given call, or are they simply wasting your time and energy?
2. Are there any commitments that are motivated merely by guilt or the approval of man?
3. Are you too busy to spend time in prayer and quiet time of refreshing with God?
4. How about your home life? Are you making dates with your spouse? Are you spending the time necessary to bond with your children?

Remember, God's desire for us is to enjoy abundant lives! It is only with a schedule free from constant stress and activity that we will have the focus and passion to experience the Second Mile life.

NOTES:

SECTION THREE // LAP TWO

Humility

Humility is a very slippery thing—just when we think we have it, we don't! We begin to feel so good about ourselves and how humble we have become, and before we know it, we've slid right back into pride. The two biggest tests in a Christian's life are failure and success. The bigger one, perhaps, is success. In moments of failure and struggle, we seem to embrace the lessons of brokenness and humility more easily. Success, however, can blind us to our own weaknesses and inflate our ideas about our level of strength.

In his book, *Finishing Strong*, Steve Farrar talks about the dangerous footing of success, comparing it to ice: "It's beautiful, it's smooth, it looks clean and cool. But there aren't many men who can walk on ice without falling flat on their faces or flat on their duffs. Too many accomplishments and too much recognition too soon can be tragic." When we begin to measure the level of our character only by our level of success, we will soon find ourselves careening down a slippery slope.

Humility is not thinking less of yourself; it is thinking of yourself less. It is daring to think large thoughts about God and small thoughts about you. John's gospel states, "He must increase, and I must decrease." The equation is simple, yet powerful. If we become less, God becomes more. When we subtract, He adds. Humility creates room for God to show up and show off in us. When we are full of ourselves, we crowd God out and give Him very little space to operate.

I Peter 5:6 says, *"Humble yourself under the mighty hand of God, and He will exalt you in due time."(NKJV)* When you place yourself under God's hand, in His time, He will place His hand under you! He will lift you up and promote you, but only after you follow the path of humility. God creates out of nothing, and until we become nothing, God cannot create in us. In addition, humility is what keeps us growing and moving forward in our relationship with Christ. It is the key to all learning. The minute you become proud in an area of your life, you become unable to be taught in that area, stunting all possible growth. Don't let pride convince you that you are an expert. Your knowledge and experience may put you in circles with some high-profile people, but make a decision to never lose the common touch.

PRAYER:

Create a clean heart in me, God, and help me to see the areas in my life in which I tend to operate in pride. Let my thoughts be Your thoughts and my attitudes Your attitudes. Today I choose to walk in grace for all people, including myself, and I keep my eyes and heart open to the ways in which I can be taught by You and those around me.

NOTES:

SECTION THREE // LAP THREE

Renewal

Very early in ministry, it seemed everyday was a whirlwind of activity as Rachel and I worked at balancing our time in ministry, marriage, and recreation. This incredibly hot, summer morning was no exception. We were tearing through our apartment trying to prepare for our dinner company, but I was desperate to get into my car. I had several meetings that day, and the moment Rachel dismissed me, I was out the door, bag of garbage in hand to put it in my back seat, so I could drive by the community dumpster on my way out of the parking lot. I had an old car that lacked air conditioning, so I was forced to bear the thick, humid heat all the way there, and to top things off, there was a really nasty smell in the air. *New Orleans can sure reek in the summer,* I thought as I raced to my destination. Luckily, I was on time for my meetings, and afterwards, I enjoyed the indoor air conditioning for a few more hours before returning home.

When I walked out to my car in the late afternoon I could not believe the odor in the air. And to my dismay, it grew more rancid as I approached my car! My windows were down and I could see a creature of some sort in my back seat, and that is when it dawned on me: I forgot to stop at the dumpster as I left my apartment! This garbage had been baking in the dense heat for hours, had attracted a rather large alley cat who generously helped himself to the muck, and now I had a soupy, putrid mess all over my back seat.

This memory came to mind recently as I was teaching a lesson on the importance of renewing the mind. So many people become Christians and start out their journey excited to become more like Jesus. They experience some success for a while, but very soon grow frustrated because of how difficult it is for them to change their bad habits. And it will be almost impossible for change to happen until they learn to change their minds. Romans 12:2 says: *"Do not conform any longer to the pattern of this world, but be transformed by the renewing of your mind. Then you will be able to test and approve what God's will is—his good, pleasing, and perfect will."* (NIV)

The key to transformation is renewing our minds because our thoughts lead us upon every path we take. Yes, our spirits are new when we become saved, but our minds remain the same. When we fail to take care of what is happening in our thought life, it is just like me leaving that bag of trash inside my car. Even if I would have been driving the finest car available, that garbage would still pollute it! When we renew our minds to the Word of God, we begin to replace the thoughts of defeat, insecurity, and fear with His promises of victory, confidence and power. This is the only way we can truly become like Jesus!

SECOND MILE STRETCHES:
1. Think about what you are thinking about! Replace the negative thoughts by confessing God's Word about that area of your life.
2. Spend time each day meditating on a scripture. On purpose, program the Word into your thought life.
3. Act on God thoughts…Ignore the negative ones. Remember, they're just thoughts.

NOTES:

SECTION THREE // LAP FOUR

Discipline

Several years ago, Rachel and I had an opportunity to travel to Sydney, Australia so we could participate in a Hillsong Church Conference. We stayed in a hotel at the Olympic Village, where the 2000 Olympic Games were held. Waking up early one morning, I contemplated staying in my warm bed or heading to the Aquatic Center to jump-start my day with a quick workout. Unable to fall back asleep, I figured I might as well do something productive, so I quietly packed up my bag and left.

When I walked into the gym at 5am, I was amazed to see the place packed with people. The pool was buzzing with life and activity as hundreds of young people were swimming laps. Out of curiosity, I walked over to one of the coaches blowing his whistle and asked what was going on. He informed me that these 14 and 15 year-olds had been there since 4:30am and were training for the Olympics. I was blown away at the discipline of all these kids! As I watched, every single one of them was giving each lap their all, unwilling to allow fatigue or laziness to lengthen their finish times.

Pursuing the Second Mile life on a daily basis will require this same kind of discipline, spiritually, physically, and emotionally. Paul wrote in 1 Corinthians 9:27: *"I discipline my body like an athlete, training it to do what it should. Otherwise, I fear that after preaching to others I myself might be disqualified."* (NLT) Like these athletes, we must on purpose choose discipline because our human nature will drift toward what is easy and resist what is difficult. When we put our lives on cruise control, we begin to coast through our tasks and end up in mediocrity, the antithesis of the Second Mile life. President Theodore Roosevelt once said, "There has never yet been a man in our history who led a life of ease whose name is worth remembering."

Men and women who intend on leaving a mark on their generation understand the value of disciplining the flesh; the result is a keen, strong spiritual power. They do not mind being stretched and pulled toward a higher standard because they know that God's stretching will always produce God's blessings in their lives as He opens up the kind of opportunities that produce exciting, eternal changes in their world.

SECOND MILE MINDSETS:

1. I look to find the tasks I have been procrastinating, and I complete them.
2. Every day, I do at least one thing that denies the desires of my flesh.
3. When prompted by the Holy Spirit to call someone, to pray for someone, or to bless someone, I act immediately.
4. I surround myself with relationships that stretch me to higher levels, will challenge any areas of mediocrity, and help me to stay God-centered in my life.

NOTES:

SECTION THREE // LAP FIVE

The Heart

To say my wife Rachel is safety conscious is as understated as saying we have a few mosquitoes down here in Louisiana during summer. Seriously, if the government found out about her, they'd be recruiting her to be in charge of Homeland Security. In the evening at my house, we lock the doors, we deadbolt them, we chain them...and then we set our high tech alarm system. Luckily, I often like to go downstairs for a midnight snack, so I have persuaded Rachel not to install the laser motion detectors similar to the ones used in the movie *Ocean's Eleven*. There have been times I will walk outside to move the trashcans to the curb and by the time I get back to Rachel's Fort Knox, the doors are already locked and the alarm is set. I can't even check the mail and get back into my own house!

I understand where she is coming from, though, because it would simply be foolish to go to bed at night with the doors and windows wide open. We'd be inviting all kind of trouble into our home. Our homes are our sanctuaries, our safe place, the center of activity and where we spend most of our time. Our families are nurtured there, all decisions are made there, and the very health of our marriages and children depend directly upon the health of our homes. We must make concerted efforts to guard this precious place with all our resources. It is the exact same way with our spiritual hearts.

Proverbs 4:23 admonishes us: *"Keep and guard your heart with all vigilance and above all that you guard, for out of it flow the springs of life."* (AMP) God tells us to guard our hearts above all that we guard because everything we need to succeed in life flows out of it: our health, our thoughts, our emotions, our dreams and desires, our capacity to love others...everything! In fact, as we pursue a Second Mile life, all of our gifts and talents required for ministry come from our hearts—along with our motives, our holiness, our discernment.

Is it any wonder the devil tries so meticulously to break in to steal, kill and destroy? He bombards us with negative imaginings, wrong thinking, doubts, and fears...all to undermine the power capable of flowing out of our hearts. We all need to be like Rachel and protect our hearts with the utmost diligence. As we read the rest of the proverb, God gives us great and practical strategies on how to guard our spiritual centers...

SECOND MILE STRETCHES:

"My son, attend to my words; consent and submit to my sayings. Let them not depart from your sight; keep them in the center of your heart. For they are life to those who find them, healing and health to all their flesh...Put away from you false and dishonest speech, and willful and contrary talk put far from you. Let your eyes look right on with fixed purpose, and let your gaze be straight before you. Consider well the path of your feet, and let all your ways be established and ordered aright. Turn not aside to the right hand or the left; remove your foot from evil." Proverbs 4:20-27 (AMP)

NOTES:

SECTION FOUR: outward

"Everybody can be great because anybody can serve. You don't have to have a college degree to serve. You don't have to make your subject and your verb agree to serve...You only need a heart full of grace—a soul generated by love."
—Martin Luther King, Jr.

CHAPTER EIGHT

Servanthood

In the Gospels, the life and ministry of Jesus Christ are marked with many highlights. We constantly see men and women who are in desperate need of His presence and willing to do just about anything to get close to Him: fighting crowds to touch the mere hem of his garment, breaking jars of expensive perfume to anoint Him, ripping holes through a roof in order to get a healing touch, climbing trees for a better look, stepping out of boats and walking on water to get to Him. Time and time again, we see people going to extreme lengths to be in close proximity to the Master. Why? What is so compelling, so drawing, so irresistible about Jesus?

Man's condition today has not changed over the centuries. We are still mixed up, messed up, and in desperate need of the presence of Jesus. Jesus is still the truth we look for, the forgiveness our souls need, the agent of change our hearts long for, and the hope we cannot live without. He is everything we have ever wanted and so much more. I believe one of the primary qualities that made Jesus so overpoweringly magnetic while He walked on this planet was that people around Him could sense He had great spiritual authority and wisdom, and yet He was still entirely available to every person. He considered himself to be operating in the greatest call a believer could possess: the role of a servant.

In the Gospel of John, chapter thirteen, there is an account that paints an incredible portrait of our Savior as a servant and gives us the color scheme of what we need to follow His example. This is the essence of the Second Mile Life. If we are to be His hands, His feet, and His heart here on earth, it is imperative we learn to emulate Jesus' generosity to serve all of mankind.

As Jesus' time on earth is drawing to a close, His sacrificial death on the Cross awaiting, He gathers His disciples for one last special meal. His closest associates have little idea of the significance of this moment (they have not yet grasped He is about to be killed), and they are about to be completely surprised by the actions of their Leader. For a long time, they have heard Jesus speak about His kingdom. In their minds, He is going to topple the existing Roman government and rightfully set up His new regime on earth—with power, property, and privilege being given to them, of course. At this point, they are not concerned about the price of the kingdom, but their positions in the kingdom.

However, Jesus' thoughts are not set on calculating a hostile takeover and world domination, at least not of this physical realm, anyway. His purpose on earth is not to construct buildings or set up bureaucracy, but to destroy the works of the devil and to redeem people. His priority has always been and will always be people. And now, it is important to Him that the disciples know how deep His love for them really is and that the power behind that love, servanthood, can sustain them for a lifetime. Jesus would now show the disciples the full extent of what it means to love people.

Jesus serves the disciples not for His benefit but for their blessing. He loves them completely, no strings attached. His desire is to teach them by example how to serve without fanfare and without recognition. *"When you give,"* He has taught them, *"don't let your left hand know what your right hand is doing."* (Matthew 6:3, NIV) In this one sentence, He confronts what is probably the most challenging part of serving others. Our flesh craves being seen and celebrated, especially when we have sacrificed something for another. I haven't met too many people who have a hard time turning down compliments, but I sure have seen people squirm when the good they do is credited to someone else! The praise and approval of men can be as addictive as any street drug. Few can resist their lure, but we cannot genuinely serve others in the spirit of Christ if we are stuffed full of ourselves. Others are best served when "self" does not get in the way, and Jesus is determined to give us a perfect example.

The Bible tells us, *"Jesus knew that the Father had given Him authority over everything and that He had come from God and would return to God."* (John 13:3, NLT) Authority over everything leaves very little outside of His control. At the snap of a finger or the nod of His head, He can command anything He wants, and the laws of nature must bend to His desire. The mantle of supreme sovereignty now rests upon the Son's shoulders. What is most remarkable is how Jesus responds to this authority His Father has given him.

Jesus uses this authority "over" to serve those "under." Instead of climbing to the top, He reaches for the bottom—the exact opposite of what most of us would do. His actions are intentional and purposeful; every movement is packed with meaning. To the disciples' surprise and eventual disapproval, Jesus does three significant things: (1) He gets up from the table, (2) takes off His robe, (3) and wraps a towel around His waist. Here is the Son of God assuming the position of a household slave, something they never expected to see!

GET UP

In preparing for a feast, it was Jewish custom for the hired servant of the house to wash the hands and feet of all the honored guests. Upon entering the upper room, the twelve apostles must have walked right past the basin and towel thinking, "Where is the servant to wash our feet? Whose responsibility was it to make sure he was here? Surely Jesus doesn't expect us to wash our own feet. We are way above that!"

However, Jesus makes the first move by getting up from the table, and in doing so, shows His disciples the importance of initiative and involvement. There is a time to *sit* at the table and a time to *get up* from the table. It takes much more energy and effort to get up from the table than it does to comfortably sit and consume everything put in front of us. As the bride of Christ, we must be careful not to sit at the table too long thinking that will make us spiritual giants—the only thing that will increase is our waistline!

> **He loves them completely, no strings attached.**

So many of us have fallen into the routine of gathering at God's table, week after week, Sunday after Sunday, to be fed the word of God, only to go home and do little or nothing with what we've just consumed. The results become obvious—instead of producing lean, strong, spiritually fit soldiers, we end up with something lazy, sloppy, unfit, and spiritually overweight. The problem isn't our diet—it's our lack of exercise!

With today's advanced technology, we have access to some of the best preaching and teaching available. We can listen to teaching tapes and CD's while driving down the road in our cars, we can download messages onto our iPods, and we can even tune in through streaming video sermons on the web. We seem to be educated way beyond our level of obedience. Jesus' example at the Last Supper still speaks loudly to us today: it takes action and involvement to get results. God expects us to do something with all the knowledge and information He has given us.

The importance of involvement has never been made more clear to me than when I was on my first trip to Washington DC. I made a special effort to visit the famous Holocaust Museum because several of my friends had gone before and came back with stories of their own emotional, life-changing experiences. I had only one afternoon to tour our nation's capital, so I devoted all four hours to this historic site. Once inside, I was completely overwhelmed. The pictures, videos, and stories were heartbreaking. Many times, I had to just stop and cry, grieving over the senseless genocide that had affected millions of innocent people. Now, all of a sudden, the history lessons—facts, dates, wars, and names—became very personal for me. It wasn't just information to memorize for a test—it was real life, some of the darkest days in humanity's history.

One of the videos talked about the role of the United States, how initially we were reluctant to get involved and slow to respond to this growing international crisis. The statement that stood out to me most was, "Our disapproval was not linked to the will to act." We were aware there was a problem, but it was far enough away to be someone else's problem...until that problem eventually knocked on our own doors. It wasn't until we were personally at risk, personally invested, that we began to fight this evil regime.

It is one thing to disapprove of injustice but quite another to involve yourself in the solution. If we stand on the sidelines and merely point our fingers at the things that are wrong, we become critics instead of catalysts for change. It is so easy to sit back, complain, and do nothing...and remain in a First Mile life. With time running short and so much hanging in the balance, we cannot afford to sit and spectate; we must embrace this crucial element of Second Mile living called servanthood! If we have any desire to see this world come to know Christ, then we must act like the Christ-ians we claim to be. Jesus tells us in Matthew 9:37, *"The harvest is truly plentiful, but the laborers are few."* (NKJV) Even with over two billion of us here on this planet claiming to be Christians, this statement unfortunately is as true today as it was then.

Jesus gets up from the supper table and models the principle of involvement not just to the twelve men who would soon be required to do the same, but also to all of us today!

THE ROBE

Once He gets up from the table, Jesus takes off His robe. The disciples watch in confusion because they understand the significance of His robe—it distinguishes Him as a rabbi. It sets Him apart from the common person and indicates His religious superiority. In setting aside His rabbinical garments, Jesus is showing the value of serving without titles. He is teaching the Twelve that performance is more important than position.

At the church where I serve, Healing Place Church, we have never put much stock into titles. From our beginning days in 1993 until now, we have always worked to get the job done and never stopped long enough to worry about what someone else calls us. We believe that the goal of advancing the kingdom is more important than whatever our current roles might be. Promoting the Gospel message is priority—our job descriptions are secondary and subject to change. Titles are irrelevant if the job is unfinished, so people who are motivated only by position or privilege will not last very long on our staff. I am so glad our pastor, Dino Rizzo, has worked so hard to ingrain this culture and way of thinking into our hearts because it helps to keep us all on task toward what is truly important...serving the lost and the hurting of our generation.

> **It is one thing to disapprove of injustice but quite another to involve yourself in the solution.**

Jesus exemplifies the humility of true servanthood by removing His robe and making Himself vulnerable to His disciples. Although He has the authority to parade in royal garments, to be surrounded by body guards and to distance Himself from His followers, He chooses to lay down those rights and experience the joys of close intimacy with His friends. This is the attitude Jesus has portrayed throughout His entire ministry. He was never too good or too busy to reach out and touch the sick and unclean, to associate with the outcast and the sinners, to stop and play with the children, or to feed the masses.

Second Mile serving will require us to lay down the pride that isolates us from others we might deem as 'less' or 'lower' than ourselves and to step toward people with authenticity and vulnerability. It will challenge us to abandon the need to promote ourselves and instead search for opportunities to advance those around us.

THE TOWEL

Removing His robe, Jesus now reaches for a towel and wraps it around His waist. He pours water into a basin, and the disciples are starting to understand what is about to happen. Their whole world begins to change as they witness the Highest of the high becoming the lowest of the low. In reluctance and humiliation, they sit in shock as the Son of God begins washing their dirty feet, the feet of men who have walked the rocky, dusty terrain of Palestine to follow Him. What is so beautiful is Jesus' complete awareness of the events that are about to unfold: Judas will betray Him, Peter will deny Him, and He alone will hang on a Cross. Not only will Jesus wash the dirt from their feet, He will also wash the sin from their hearts.

Jesus also realizes something about the apostles they do not yet grasp. Although these same feet will run away in fear, they will return in power, and Jesus will require these feet to go the Second Mile—to go the distance, serve sacrificially, and take the Gospel to the world.

Outside of the Cross, this moment stands as one of the most compelling acts of love man could ever know—the righteousness and the purity of heaven coming in contact with the filth and the sinfulness of man. Jesus was not afraid to get messy and involve Himself in our broken world.

The call to lay down our titles and to pick up our towels still rings loudly today. The texture of Second Mile living is not silk or rayon emblazoned with a trendy logo—it is a towel. This towel will confront our insecurities and test our motives as we embrace the call to serve the lost, the hurting, and the unloved. The pathway to Kingdom greatness is not paved with awards or trophies, it comes only by way of the towel; there are no other short cuts or alternatives. In Mark 10:42-45 Jesus says: *"You know that those who are regarded as rulers of the Gentiles lord it over them, and their high officials exercise authority over them. Not so with you. Instead, whoever wants to become great among you must be your servant, and whomever wants to be first must be slave of all. For even the Son of Man did not come to be served, but to serve, and to give his life as a ransom for many."(NIV)*

This is why God has placed us on the map. My pastor reminds us constantly, "We exist to serve the poor and hurting in our communities in a thousand different ways, otherwise, we just become expensive institutions." I don't want Jesus to look back at our churches and say, "You cost Me so much but you produced so little." Our leaders must be sent out into our neighborhoods with a Bible in one hand and a towel in the other. We can preach the message "Jesus saves" best when we serve those in our communities that are considered the least.

When we choose to serve others in the spirit of Christ, we put the goodness of God on display. We become the light that penetrates darkness and catches the attention of others. Jesus said, *"Don't hide your light under a basket! Instead, put it on a stand and let it shine for all. In the same way, let your good deeds shine out for all to see, so that everyone will praise your heavenly Father." (Matthew 5:15-16, NLT)* Did you notice the method of evangelism Jesus describes in the above verses? People will ultimately be brought to a place of praise and adoration of Christ, not because our preaching is so eloquent but because our serving is so effective.

As you read this book, consider the light you are now using. It may be a lamp on a nightstand, a light switch in a bedroom, or even sunlight outside. Regardless of the source, the light is silent—it makes no noise. It just quietly and consistently pushes back the darkness and enables you to see. A high impact church is the same way. It places greater value on actions than it does on empty words. Our words will only be effective to the degree that our lives match our message. Acts of kindness and good works serve as beacons of light in this spiritually dark world, illuminating a path that helps people find their way. Kindness is a language spoken by all tribes and all peoples. A blind man can see it, a deaf man can hear, and a lost man can feel it.

THE PAYOFF

As Jesus brings this powerful lesson to a close, He asks them, *"Do you understand what I was doing? You call me 'Teacher' and 'Lord,' and you are right, because it is true. And since I, the Lord and Teacher have washed your feet, you ought to wash each other's feet. I have given you an example to follow...You know these things—now do them! This is the path of blessing." (John 13:12-15, 17, NLT)*

Jesus gives them the formula for a life of radical blessing and favor:

Knowing + Doing = Blessing

I have not met a single person who wants to go through life without the blessings of God. We pray for His blessings daily on our marriages, our homes, our children, our businesses, and everything our hand touches. But so many of us want the blessings of God without ever paying a price for them. We want to simply confess God's Word and wait for the blessings of healing and prosperity to rain on down! While God's promises are true, and a confession of faith will bring results, this kind of First Mile living will never become saturated with the kind of rich blessings Jesus was referring to in the Book of John.

Second Mile Christians are not fulfilled to simply act as benchwarmers in church, or to watch as bystanders while others get in the game and enjoy the excitement of participating in the ministry of Jesus. There is no gratification in our hearts to merely receive; this only brings an aftertaste of dissatisfaction. We long to emulate Christ, to make ourselves available to those around us and to witness transformation in their lives as they come to know the saving power of Jesus. We are not intimidated to love and to serve those whom the world has forgotten, and unlike the world, we seek no accolades or material rewards when we do so. We are in passionate pursuit of the incomparable thrill and joy that only Second Mile servanthood can offer.

CHAPTER NINE

The Invitation

Wow! This Christian life I am living is so far beyond what I have ever imagined, I thought as I hurriedly drove away from work. I could not wait to get home to tell Rachel about what had just happened. Slowing down for traffic, I was given the time to digest the events of the day, and in the process I remembered the journey home I described in the first chapter of this book. What a different feeling I was experiencing today than that day! Then, I was dealing with such dissatisfaction inside, wondering when the time would come that I would know my life was making a real difference. And today it seemed as if with every turn I made, God was blowing me away with another opportunity to affect the life of someone around me. No more was there that vacancy in my heart; rather, the fulfillment I had within sometimes was almost overwhelming. Like at this moment...

There was a woman I had come across through ministry who was walking through an incredibly devastating season. About a year earlier, she had found out that her husband had been molesting her children behind her back. Immediately, she took legal action, and the man was now serving the beginning of a long prison sentence, but the damage had been done and her family was sifting through the aftermath. One child, now a teenager would be found cutting herself and trying to commit suicide, an outward manifestation of how devalued she felt, and the other was so angry he was acting out and causing himself to be expelled from every school in town. To make matters worse, this family was in financial ruin to the point they had to declare bankruptcy.

One day, I received a call from this woman, crying and desperate. She explained to me that although she had completely repainted and redecorated their home, the horrible memories of what had happened there seemed to haunt all of them. "These walls speak of only terrible things, and we have to move out of this house. So, I found an apartment, met with the owners and applied for tenancy, and they assured me all would be fine. But I just received a call from them, and because of my bankruptcy, the application has been denied. I didn't know where else to turn, Pastor Mike. Can you help me?!"

What am I going to be able to do? I thought. And then I felt God speak to my heart, *What can you do?* The only thing I could think of was to try giving the owners of the complex a call, not that I could imagine how that was going to help. Nevertheless, I asked her for the number, and promised her I would do everything I could.

I was nervous to make the call because I had no idea what I was going to say, but I had given her my word. When the young woman answered the phone, I took a breath and just started to talk. "Hi. You don't know me, but my name is Mike Haman, and I'm one of the pastors at Healing Place Church. Just a few minutes ago, I—"

"Mike?!" interrupted the young woman. "Mike Haman? This is Jenny!"

"Excuse me?" I said, as I was not expecting this reaction.

"It's Jenny. You used to live in Rosemont Apartments, right?"

Then it all clicked. This was a young girl who lived by Rachel and me a few years earlier.

"JENNY! Girl, whasssup? How have you been?!"

The next few minutes were such a relief to me as she asked me all about Rachel and the kids, and I inquired about her family. After we caught up, I proceeded to tell her the story of this woman and her kids.

"Jenny, she just needs a new start and a safe place for her kids. Is there anything at all you can do?" She told me she would call the owners and get back to me. Not ten minutes later, my phone rang to Jenny's voice saying, "You tell that precious woman to pack their bags and come move into their new apartment on Monday."

After thanking Jenny profusely for her help, I began to call the woman back to tell her the great news, but God once again spoke to my heart, *Is that all you can do?* I sat for a moment and knew this was an invitation to go deeper into the Second Mile. I got an idea and began to get to work. About an hour later, I experienced one of the greatest privileges of my pastoral life as I called this woman who so desperately was trying to put the pieces of her family's life back together.

> **The lost and the hurting are not waiting for the next great sermon.**

"I'm so sorry for the delay in getting back to you," I said, "But I want you to pack all of your belongings because on Monday morning, we are sending to your house several trucks and about a dozen strong men to help all of you move into your new apartment!"

As this woman wept on the phone, I tried my best to keep my composure as she thanked me repeatedly. All I could say to her was it was God Who had made the way, not me, and that He deserved all the thanks. When I hung up the phone, I was in a daze at the wondrous love and mercy of Jesus, Who always will make a way for the hurting and the oppressed...if His people will answer the invitation to be His mouth, hands and feet. As I left my office to share this awesome experience with Rachel, I humbly thanked God for allowing me to be a part of His plan of healing for this family, and for the tremendous feeling of fulfillment this life in the Second Mile offered. *Keep 'em coming, Lord,* I prayed. *This excitement and sense that my life is truly making a difference will never, ever get old!*

IT'S FOR EVERYONE

This story is a great example of the Second Mile life. I share it, not to bring praise to myself, but to set forth a vision of what types of opportunities are available to you and every other Christian who will make the choice to go off-roading into the Second Mile. The lost and the hurting are not waiting for the next great sermon; they need to be ministered to and if we will silence the influence of our selfish society and get quiet on the inside, we will notice the sounds of our Savior. We will hear His call to go the Second Mile in our families, in our workplaces, and throughout our communities. The clock is ticking and God-moments are waiting all around us. In such urgent times, and with so much ground to gain, we cannot afford to drag our feet or to walk away.

There is a story in the Gospel of Mark of a young man who was invited by Jesus Himself to enter into a higher level of living he had never known before. But because of his small-minded, selfish thinking, he perceived the invite to be loss instead of the incredible gain Christ was offering him, and he walked away. It's the famous account of the rich young ruler in Mark 10:17-31. This man came running to Jesus and knelt before Him, inquiring how he could go deeper in his spiritual walk. He was obviously very hungry and eager for the things of God as this affluent leader humbled himself before His Lord.

There must have been some level of relationship between Jesus and the man because the Bible makes a point to say that Jesus loved him. After a brief exchange, Jesus cuts to the chase and speaks candidly: *"One thing you lack: Go your way, sell whatever you have and give to the poor, and you will have treasure in heaven; and come take up the cross, and follow Me." But he was sad at this word, and went away sorrowful, for he had great possessions.* (Mark 10:21-22, NKJV)

Jesus must have been disappointed at the young man's reaction, but He did not chase him down to further explain what He meant or to persuade him to change his mind. He simply turned to His disciples and commented how difficult it is for those who put their trust in the things of the world to enter into the kingdom of God. The disciples were astonished. How could Jesus let this man of prestige, wealth and influence simply walk away? He would have been a superior asset to their ministry. But the rich ruler disqualified himself because he did not have the ears to hear the fullness of what Jesus was offering him; he merely understood the invitation to mean the giving up of the things he held dear and the loss of an easy life filled with security and comfort.

Many Christians today have this same perspective. They see the call of Christ to be one of loss: loss of money, loss of freedom, loss of personal desires, loss of comfort. So they stay in the First Mile, safe and secure in the knowledge that one day they will see heaven and they never look up to see all the people in their sphere of influence who will spend their eternities separated from God.

> **His purposes for our lives will ultimately never lead us into lack.**

They ignore the ache inside their spirits to affect their world and convince themselves they are holding on to what is precious...they have no idea what they are missing. And Jesus does not chase them down trying to manipulate or persuade them to think otherwise. He gives the call, and he who has ears to hear will answer.

Peter, ever seeking to fully understand what Jesus had to say, pursues a greater explanation from Him. *"See, we have left all and followed You."* So Jesus answered and said, *"Assuredly, I say to you, there is no one who has left house or brothers or sisters or father or mother or wife or children or lands, for My sake and the gospel's who shall not receive a hundredfold now in this time—houses and brothers and sisters and mothers and children and lands, with persecutions—and in the age to come, eternal life."* (vs. 28-30, NKJV)

If only the rich, young ruler had not given up his pursuit for a higher spiritual life so soon, he would have heard Jesus reassuring His followers that whenever a person gives anything up for the sake of the Gospel, he receives from God one hundredfold in this life on earth! Yes, it might come with some sacrifice and persecution from the world, but Jesus came that we might have an abundant life! His purposes for our lives will ultimately never lead us into lack. If that ruler would have sold all his possessions, the only thing he would have lost is his greed and dependence upon earthly things. He then would have been free to receive the true prosperity of selfless wealth.

What is the 'one thing you lack' that is preventing you from a total surrender to the call of Christ to passionately pursue the Second Mile life? Are you like the rich young ruler and afraid to give up what is comfortable? Are you worried God will ask you to do something you won't like? Psalm 37:4 promises: *"Delight yourself also in the Lord and He will give you the desires of your heart."* (NIV) Are you afraid you won't be able to do it? Philippians 4:13 says: *"I can do all things through Christ who strengthens me."* (NIV) Are you simply afraid? 2 Timothy encourages: *"God did not give you a spirit of fear, but one of power and of love and of a sound mind."* (NKJV) No matter what the 'one thing you lack' is, I guarantee there is a promise in God's Word that will dispel that lie and give you the courage, compassion, and strength to embrace Christ's call within you to go deeper with Him than you have ever gone before.

Going the Second Mile is not merely an event or even a series of good deeds; rather, it is a mentality that influences everything you do. It is marked by a continuous, on-purpose movement toward Christ-likeness. Your heart will be expanded by it. Your marriage will be changed by it. Your children will be drawn to it. Your friendships will grow because of it. Your career will benefit from it. And most of all, the kingdom of God will be advanced through it.

The pursuit of this kind of lifestyle will confront your past experiences, bringing the freedom and healing you have yearned for. It will open up your eyes to your current realities, helping you to eradicate mediocrity and apathy. It will focus your vision and path toward your future hopes and dreams. It will stretch you beyond what you think is possible and invigorate you with the accomplishment of greater works than you ever imagined for yourself.

The journey of the Second Mile simply begins with the first step. If you are longing for more in your Christian life and are growing restless with where you are right now, it is time for you to step out. You may feel like you are going in circles—the scenery always looking the same. If you want something you have never had, you must do something you have never done. Refuse to shrink back from this invitation because you believe it to be too daunting, for the Spirit of God will give you the strength you need to put one foot in front of the other.

Once you experience the joy and wonder of Second Mile living, you will never want to go back to the First Mile stuff you used to know. You will question how you ever made it living below the level of what God has designed for you, and you will not only spend each day excitedly looking for every opportunity to bless and to serve others, but you will also long to bring others with you on this journey. The Second Mile will not always be easy, but it will certainly be thrilling, fulfilling and overflowing with blessings beyond your wildest dreams.

The time to answer the call is now...Jesus is waiting for you with His hand extended to work His wonders through you. Let go of the lower life with all its supposed comforts and surrender yourself to God's higher life of the unpredictable, of the miraculous, of the supernatural...of the Second Mile.

EVERY LAP COUNTS

SECTION FOUR // LAP ONE

Finishing Strong

In 2 Timothy 4:7, the Apostle Paul writes: *I have fought the fight, I have finished the race, and I have remained faithful.* (NLT) After having been stoned almost to death several times, beaten and whipped, imprisoned in terrible conditions, shipwrecked, ridiculed and abandoned, all for the cause of Christ, this statement of Paul's is amazing. Most of us would have given up after the first stoning, let alone multiple ones. Paul was not just a Second Miler, but a Third, Fourth and Eighty-Seventh Miler!

Have you ever noticed how good we are at starting things and how not so good we are at finishing them? Usually this is because the genesis of our task was fueled by feelings like excitement, happiness, and even guilt. But while emotions may help us start things, they rarely sustain us to finish them. At the beginning of every New Year, we are motivated to diligently map out goals, identify the changes we want to make, and construct elaborate strategies designed to bring certain success. January One, we go on diets, join health clubs, set budgets, and begin our read-the-Bible-through-in-a-year challenge...and then somewhere in March, we have trashed the diet, abandoned the gym, overspent, and gotten lost in the book of Leviticus for the third straight year!

The only way to cross the finish line of our goals is to stay committed even when the fuel of our emotions has run out. We will get way more mileage out of commitment than we ever will out of emotions.

SECOND MILE STRATEGIES:

1. Pick one area you want to work on, and set a reasonable goal—never try to change everything all at once!
2. Find scriptures in the Bible you can confess over yourself, and use your faith as a tool of motivation when it starts to get difficult.
3. Keep yourself accountable. Tell a good friend about your goals and ask them to check in with you from time to time about your progress.
4. Use the power of the Holy Spirit within you! Remember, you can do all things through Christ who strengthens you.

NOTES:

SECTION FOUR // LAP TWO

Relationships that Build

Not to sound like Forrest Gump or anything, but 'my momma always used to say,' there are four kinds of people in this world: those who add, those who subtract, those who multiply, and those who divide. Connect yourself with those who add and multiply the goodness of God in your life...avoid those who subtract and divide. She understood the proverb: *Whoever walks with the wise will become wise; whoever walks with fools will suffer harm. (Proverbs 13:20, NLT)*

Our success in life will be determined by the people around us and their influence upon our hearts. If we surround ourselves with small-minded, negative people, then no matter how much we want to achieve great things for the Kingdom, we will be weighed down by their attitudes of doubt and fear. On the other hand, if we surround ourselves with men and women who are faith-filled, positive, generous people, we will always feel energized and encouraged in their presence. Walking through life with these types of Christians enable us to believe in our dreams when the horizon seems foggy and to muster up the courage and the 'God' strength necessary to accomplish them.

In addition, strong Christian relationships provide borders for us as we navigate through the temptations of life by providing accountability. When we opened our lives up to friends who share the same principles as we do, we are much less likely to 'all of a sudden' find ourselves entangled in a web of sin. Not only will they be able to sense when we are hiding something from them, but also, they will ask the direct questions we need at those times of temptation. Second Milers understand the importance and the necessity of close friendships and we pursue to build relationships that build. We lock arms with those who are of the same spirit and are of like faith.

SCRIPTURES TO MEDITATE ON:

Proverbs 27:17 As iron sharpens iron, So a man sharpens the countenance of his friend. (NKJV)

Proverbs 18:1 He who willfully separates and estranges himself from God and man seeks his own desire and rages against all wise and sound judgment. (AMP)

2 Corinthians 6:14 Don't team up with those who are unbelievers. How can goodness be a partner with wickedness? How can light live with darkness? (NLT)

NOTES:

SECTION FOUR // LAP THREE

Refresh Yourself

"Those who wait for the Lord, who expect, look for, and hope in Him shall renew their strength and power; they shall lift their wings and mount up close to God as eagles mount up to the sun; they shall run and not be weary, they shall walk and not faint or become tired." Isaiah 40:31 (AMP)

God needs us to be around for the long haul. This race is not about getting to the end of our lives as fast as possible, it is about living full lives of abundance and quality that bring glory to God. This cannot happen if we are so exhausted and 'run-ragged' that we find ourselves crawling toward our finish line like a dehydrated man in a parched desert. But life comes at us fast, and unless we purpose in our hearts to take time to slow down and refresh ourselves, we'll never be able to thrive through the Second Mile life...we'll only be surviving.

We live in a world addicted to speed and acceleration. Our cars have engines that move them faster. Our computers have chips that increase their speed and reduce our time of waiting. Even our coffee has to be ready in an instant. We suffer from a disease called urgentitis, and it's an epidemic. If we do not vaccinate ourselves from this world virus by spending time in the presence of God, our spirits will begin to become very weak, and our souls will be open to all types of temptations. In addition, we will form a lifestyle that moves so fast, we will merely skim over the surface of life and never experience the richness and the depth of the life God planned for us. Sometimes we just need to slow down, put on the breaks, and call a time-out!

The great tragedy in life is not what men suffer—it's what they miss. Speed has a clever way of robbing us…let's not speed through life missing what's most important. The relationships we never deepen… the people we never serve…the prayers we never pray…the spiritual conversations we never have…the gifts we never give…the spiritual gifts we never exercise…the battles we never fight…the victories we never win…the tears we never cry…all because we're in such a hurry.

You and I were made for so much more. Let's not just race through our lives; let's enjoy it!

SECOND MILE STRETCHES:

1. Stop. Sit. Breathe. Focus into the presence of God…DAILY. If you find this difficult, then you are exactly who I'm talking to!
2. When you find yourself caught in traffic, instead of giving in to the tightness in your chest, use the time to relax and talk to God. The world has never ended because a person happened to be late.
3. Do you have a hobby of any kind? An activity that allows you to shut off your mind from your job, your ministry, your 'worries?' Make sure you are making the time to simply 'shut off' and regenerate your soul.

NOTES:

SECTION FOUR // LAP FOUR

Take Responsibility

Jesus was the master at taking responsibility. The Gospels are packed with hundreds of examples of Him seeing a need and filling it. He didn't look around to see if there was anyone else to do the job or stop to think about what others might think; if He saw someone who was experiencing lack and seeking in their hearts a way of escape, He immediately went in to action. He was fully aware of His power and authority to handle any situation and He never hesitated to answer the cry of a person in need to the point of taking the responsibility of the sin of humanity upon the cross!

Where would we all be today had Jesus not stepped up to the plate? I cannot even imagine the oppressive darkness that all of humanity would be experiencing if there was not the Hope of Christ anywhere on this planet. Because Jesus took the ultimate responsibility for our sin and our eternal lives, there are about 2 billion people today who claim to believe in Him and who will be privileged to embrace an eternal relationship with God in heaven. What about the other approximately 4.5 billion? Who will take responsibility for them?

It's up to you and me. In the first chapter of John, it describes Jesus as light, the One True Light that had come into the world. Then in Matthew 5, Jesus calls us the light. Throughout the Bible, there are many words describing the power and the attributes of Jesus: the Way, the Truth, the Shepherd, the Word, the Son, the Alpha and Omega, the

Door, the Messiah, and the list goes on. But here, Jesus actually calls us the same thing He calls Himself: The Light. What an incredible privilege and responsibility…if we will dare to embrace it!

Living in the Second Mile is all about taking responsibility. Taking responsibility to be Christ in the earth, to be His Light shining brightly into the lives of those trapped in darkness, and to continue His ministry of destroying the works of the devil. Jesus has given us His Name, accompanied with His authority, and as a result, we have been fully equipped to storm this world for Christ. All it takes is a Second Mile courage to take responsibility and answer the call!

SECOND MILE MINDSETS:

1. It is up to me to spread the light of the Gospel to those around me. I look for every open door to share my testimony with my friends, my loved ones, and my co-workers.
2. If I see someone in need, and I have it within my ability to meet that need, I do not delay or look around to see if someone else will respond first.
3. I live my life by the motto of St. Francis of Assisi: "At all times, I preach the Gospel, and when necessary, I use words."

NOTES:

SECTION FOUR // LAP FIVE

Enter into the Second Mile

1. Put down this book.

2. Go out into the mission field of your neighborhood, community, and country with a purpose to be a shining light.

3. Become an active participant in the race of life and passionately pursue the lost so they might come to understand the saving knowledge of Jesus Christ!

About the Author

Mike Haman is the Teaching Pastor at Healing Place Church, as well as the Administrator of Student Ministries. He also serves as the pastor of the college and young professionals' gathering, and presides as the Dean of the Elevate School of Ministry.

Mike has a passionate desire to empower people in the local church to live the life that God intended. God has given him a vibrant gift to effectively communicate and teach biblical principles for daily living, equipping people to discover their calling and embrace their purpose.

With more than a decade of experience in ministry and leadership, Mike has had opportunities to share the relevant and timeless gospel message in many venues. He preaches at NFL chapels, on college campuses throughout the country, and internationally in places such as India, Africa, Italy, Sri Lanka and Honduras.

Mike's heart is fully committed to his family. He lives in Prairieville, Louisiana with his wife Rachel, their two daughters, Alexa and Mikaela, and their son, Trevor.

HEALINGPLACECHURCH
A HEALING PLACE FOR A HURTING WORLD

REACH · SERVE
GIVE · BUILD

Come join us at Healing Place Church for exciting worship, relevant Biblical teachings, and great age appropriate activities that your kids will love!

LEAD PASTORS
DINO & DELYNN RIZZO

VISIT OUR HIGHLAND CAMPUS
19202 HIGHLAND ROAD · BATON ROUGE, LA · 70809

SERVICE TIMES
SATURDAYS: 5:00pm
SUNDAYS: 8:00am, 10:00am, 12:00pm
WEDNESDAYS: 7:00pm

CALL US
225.753.2273

VISIT US ONLINE
WWW.HEALINGPLACECHURCH.ORG

ALSO FROM HEALING PLACE CHURCH

TURNING POINTS by Dino Rizzo

The road of life is often paved with hardships, tragedy, personal loss, and disappointment. Too often, we find ourselves trapped in one of these moments, desperately searching for a way out. In Turning Points, Dino Rizzo tells how God can use these moments to be turning points in our lives. If we'll trust him, He'll guide us through our challenges, and we'll start to enjoy the incredible plan He has for us.

This book is a must read for anyone who is either struggling with the issue of Christ in their life, or the believer who is in the midst of one of life's turning points. This book will help bring the peace of God and allow His plan to take root in your life, so that you can live the victorious life that He intended you to live.

I AM NOT FORGOTTEN a Series by HPC

Have you ever felt overlooked, passed over, and forgotten? When tragedy strikes, when someone abandons us, we feel completely forgotten.

In "I Am Not Forgotten", Lead Pastor Dino Rizzo delivers a message from God for every man, woman and child: some may not remember you, others may overlook you, but you are not forgotten. God remembers you! He is right there with you as you face every storm and trial. Through good times and bad, He is standing by your side. He knows your name. You are precious to God! In this 6-Part series, our hope is that you hear God's promise that He will never leave you nor forsake you and discover your place in God's heart.

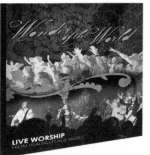

WONDER OF THE WORLD CD/DVD Set

This latest recording from Healing Place Music effectively captures the heart of the passionate worshippers that filled the sanctuary that incredible night. This CD/DVD combo is merely a reflection of our love for our Father in Heaven, as well as our appreciation for all of His gifts, inspirations, and His continuous grace and mercy. This album was recorded in the midst of a very trying time in our community and surrounding areas. Our prayer is that the light of God would bring hope to all who are hurting both here and abroad, and that through this recording all would discover Jesus Christ, the true Wonder of the World. Get your copy today!

for more information visit www.healingplacechurch.org